To Marzial

HMOs

COMPENSATION FOR

UNLAWFUL EVICTION

An Insider's Guide to Legal Battles
Over Unlawful Eviction

C. J. Haliburton, BA DMS CERT Ed
Also known as HMO Daddy

Best of luck

07554452790

www.hmodaddy.com

HMO Daddy
14 Walsall Road
Wednesbury
West Midlands
WS10 9JL

Print Edition
ISBN: 978-1-326-12564-6

British Library Cataloguing in Publication Data.

A catalogue record for this book is available from the British Library.

Design, editing and formatting by Oxford Literary Consultancy.

Disclaimer

Note, all material provided in this book is for informational purposes only, and may not be suitable for your needs or goals. Please consult a qualified advisor to assist you.

Testimonials

"When reading this book, my jaw dropped a couple of times. Some of the cases are truly shocking! It's a wonder that anyone dares to be a landlord. Essential reading for anyone who owns property."

Stephanie J. Hale – author of Millionaire Women, Millionaire You

Contents

Introduction

I recently had a case brought against me for unlawful eviction by an HMO (House in Multiple Occupation) tenant. It was actually the first case brought against me by any tenant. When I got to court, I realised I was looking at a possible compensation claim which costs in the region of £100,000. Thankfully, I won and the tenant lost. I had little experience in this area and could not find any guidance to help me learn what it was all about. So I performed a bit of research and these are the cases I found regarding mainly HMO tenants, also known as room lets.

I have published this book filled with cases for HMO landlords, to bring home the seriousness (and risks) of evicting tenants. This book will also explain the proper legal procedures, as well as the problems with abandonments, so you know what to watch out for to avoid being sued. The gravity by which the courts treat unlawful eviction is summed up in Drane v Evangelou 1978 by Lord Justice Lawton:

'To deprive a man of a roof over his head, in my judgment, is one of the worst torts (wrongs) which can be committed. It causes stress, worry and anxiety.'

L.J Lawton must have lived a very closeted life if he believed this was the worst thing that could happen to someone. Try sexual abuse of children and adults, personal injury, etc.

HMO tenants enjoy the same protection as single-let tenants. This is often nonsense because HMO tenants are in the main transient, treating the property more as a guesthouse rather than a permanent home, but I did not write the law.

Enjoy, learn and above all beware! Much of what landlords have got themselves into in this book seems to be down to ignorance and frustration with the legal process. If you understand how that process works, it will help you to avoid having the same problems.

If you wish to get a quick overview of the excesses of the system, I suggest that you read the following three cases first:

Walsh v Shuangyan: 2010

Oxford City Council v Kenston McIntosh: 2010

Abbas v Iqbal: 2009

C. J. Haliburton

HMO Daddy has written a manual on how to evict tenants yourself, and also runs courses on eviction which show you how to simply, quickly, cheaply and legally evict tenants with any rent arrears without the need for expensive lawyers.

Please visit my website www.hmodaddy.com

How is Compensation for Unlawful Eviction Calculated?

The general aim of compensation is to put tenants into the position that they would have been in if there had been no unlawful eviction. However, exemplary damages are awarded against the landlord to stop them from profiting from their action. For example, saving the cost of evicting through the court and being able to charge a higher rent to a new tenant or make a profit from developing the property.

Tenants bringing about civil proceedings following acts of harassment or unlawful eviction may be entitled to five different categories of damages:

1. Special damages

These are compensation for any identifiable loss that is quantifiable in monetary terms. Some examples include the loss of earnings, second-hand value of lost items (usually clothes and other personal possessions), additional costs of meals, cost of alternative accommodation, etc. Any expenditure should be reasonable, proper, and necessary.

2. General damages

This is compensation for losses that are not quantifiable in monetary terms. Some examples include discomfort, inconvenience, loss of enjoyment, loss of occupation, shock, personal injury, pain and suffering. The courts generally award a whopping £100 to £300 per night to an HMO tenant who has had to sleep rough due to being unlawfully evicted. The courts do not seem to distinguish between an HMO tenant living in a room, which is often looked upon as temporary, and a family living in a house they have made their home. This seems like a lot of money when you consider an HMO tenant is generally only paying £50 to £100 for the room. When you compare this to being deprived of your liberty, a victim does not get anywhere near this level of compensation for being wrongly imprisoned, but the state is generally paying this compensation to persons who have been wrongfully convicted of a crime.

3. Aggravated damages

This is compensation for severe suffering or to demonstrate the outrage and indignation at the way a person has been treated. They are compensatory in nature and reflect the victim's suffering when a tenant is physically and publicly thrown out of their home.

4. Exemplary damages

These are punitive and are awarded to punish or deter a defendant. They may be awarded when the defendant's (landlord's) behaviour was calculated to make a profit. Exemplary damages are not confined to money-making in the strictest sense. Obtaining possession without the trouble and expense of going to court falls within this category and the courts believe it would cost between £1,000 to £2,000 to employ a solicitor to evict, so they award this amount for not following the legal route for eviction. I wonder if any of these judges have ever had to pay to have a solicitor evict a tenant since this amount seems low.

5. Nominal damages

These are awarded in respect of those wrongs where it is not necessary to show that damage has occurred (e.g. trespass to land, goods or person, which means moving or touching them).

NB: Judges occasionally get these damages muddled up.

6. Costs

What's missing with all the following cases are the legal costs. Even if you represent yourself and lose, you will still be liable for the claimant's costs along with the compensation awarded to the tenant. These costs will start at about £10,000 but are often a lot, lot more! The problem is that you have no way of quantifying the costs if you lose, or before you start.

The best advice is to settle before these costs rack up. Since Legal Aid has been withdrawn, the claimant (tenant) will usually have a 'No Win No Fee' solicitor where the legal costs are covered by insurance. When insurance is involved, the legal costs can be doubled should the claimant win.

In the past, most of the claimants would have been Legally Aided; the case reports do not refer to this. The problem with Legal Aid is that the tenant does not usually have to pay a penny for it. With unlawful eviction, if you lost then you could not claim your costs against the Legal Aid fund and the tenants were not worth suing to recover your costs. So if you won, it still cost you.

The new system seems even worse for encouraging spurious claims. The solicitor gets insurance to cover their costs so they are paid whether they lose or win, and the tenant does not have to pay a penny for bringing the case to court.

I recently spoke to a landlady who was sued by an ex-tenant over the loss of the tenant's possessions. She finally ended up settling (after the case was adjourned three times) for £7,500 to compensate the tenant for his alleged loss of possessions, which she claimed was just a pile of rubbish the cleaner had thrown away. The costs were about £50,000 – this included both hers and the tenant's costs. She was represented by a solicitor, whereas the tenant's costs were covered by legal costs insurance so they doubled. She had to pay this fee as part of the settlement.

The landlady involved regretted not settling at the beginning. It was not only the money, it was all the stress that she was forced to endure. On the other hand, the tenant had nothing to worry about since his costs were being funded by insurance and there would be no consequences for him if he lost, apart from not being compensated for a load of rubbish he left behind and the time and trouble of finding a solicitor who would take his case.

How to Avoid Liability

Unlawful eviction and many other areas of law have resulted in a hidden industry where businesses are blackmailed in secret by unscrupulous streetwise litigants and dubious lawyers. All a tenant has to do is allege they have been unlawfully evicted by a landlord who is not savvy to the ramifications of what they do. The tenant will then be aided by a solicitor who will happily represent them for an eye-watering fee, either paid for by the Legal Aid Fund or by insurers (as Legal Aid has been withdrawn from his type of case). The landlord will then go to their solicitor who will give what is considered the best advice, which is to settle. After reviewing the cases in this book, you will probably agree that this may be the best thing to do. How many millions or billions of pounds are being extorted by this means is a hidden secret. Lawyers, who have become the main beneficiaries, are unlikely to expose this hidden gravy train and I see no one standing up for landlords.

The only advice I can give is to know the rules of the game and know what you are up against. Never refuse to let a tenant return to the property who alleges they have been evicted without the proper procedure which is:

1. Surrender – the tenant leaves and returns the keys. I always advise to get this in writing, signed and dated by the tenant. I supply such a form, without liability, in my *HMO Forms and Notices* manual. (Available on USB and CD) See my website www.hmodaddy.com for details.

OR

2. Court possession order, which costs money and takes months. Then if the tenant has still not left, the court bailiff is used to evict them.

I find society's approach to most Local Housing Allowance tenants and criminals as strange. I am not saying all Local Housing Allowance tenants are criminals. It is a fact that most convicted criminals are on Local Housing Allowance. Nor am I stating that most crime is committed by those on Local Housing Allowance. It is that they are the ones who are mostly convicted.

Criminals are sometimes treated harshly and can be imprisoned as a punishment. Prison seems to be remarkably ineffective since over 70% of prisoners who are released end up back in prison. It is often said by those in favour of prison that it works 30% of the time but I have grave doubts about this and suspect that most of that 30% would not have committed another offence anyway. Possibly, if many of the other 70% had been treated differently, then they may not go on to committing more criminal offences.

Once an ex-criminal is released from prison, they are given the title of 'vulnerable' and some will actually use their accommodation as a base for crime. In my experience, they will use it for drug dealing, prostitution and theft, often causing an enormous amount of damage to the landlord's property. This damage is ignored by the council's Tenancy Support Officers who often vigorously enforce the tenant's 'rights' and turn a blind eye to the effects these tenants are having on the locality and other tenants and provide no help or support for landlords.

In such circumstances, you can understand why many landlords are very reluctant to house such tenants.

How to Legally Evict a Tenant

How do you evict a tenant? If you follow the court route, the law is too slow to be of much commercial use and it is a bureaucratic mess. I will give a brief outline of the legal process to evict.

The Legal Process

There are legally only two ways to remove a tenant:

1. If the tenant voluntarily gives up their tenancy – this is known as a surrender.

2. By order of the court – which incurs costs and can take over 16 weeks to go through, providing no defence is filed.

Any other way and you risk an action for either illegal or unlawful eviction. The difference between illegal and unlawful eviction is that illegal eviction is criminal, so you risk being fined and/or going to prison. Illegal evictions are usually enforced by the council's Housing Department and the police have even been known to prosecute. Unlawful eviction is civil, which means the tenant has to instigate legal action via a solicitor or a legal help centre such as the Citizens' Advice Bureau. However, if the tenant is capable, they can sue themselves. The result of a successful action for unlawful eviction is that you could end up paying a substantial amount in compensation to the tenant. Furthermore, let's not forget the civil and criminal offence of harassment; you don't even need to evict a tenant to run foul of this. Harassment is defined very widely, and is anything which interferes with the tenant's *"quiet enjoyment of their tenancy"*.

The law is one-sided, all on the tenant's side. If a landlord had to use the court every time they evict a non-paying tenant who refused to leave, it would make renting an unviable option. As a solicitor once said to me in a very cheerful way, "There is nothing to stop a tenant refusing to pay their rent, once they have moved in. It will take over six months, if you act quickly and are lucky, to evict them." I think he was seriously considering refusing to pay his own rent!

My Experience

I always use eviction as the last resort when all else fails. As a landlord, I provide help in claiming housing benefits and warn tenants about their behaviour before considering eviction. If a tenant leaves, I usually have to clean up the room, find another tenant and have a void period. It's often better to try and make the best of what you have than to find another tenant.

The amount of problems that a landlord can have depends on the type of tenants they have. No sector is immune but in my experience, I have had very few problems with professional tenants and a lot more with unemployed tenants. How you deal with the tenants depends on who they are.

The majority of my tenants live in what most people would call bedsits and are blue collar workers or unemployed. I get rid of most of my non-paying and troublesome tenants by asking them to leave. In most cases, it's as simple as that! I find many inexperienced landlords find this odd, are disbelieving, and reluctant to do it themselves. It takes practice to perfect the skill of asking a defaulting tenant to leave, nerves of steel, patience and complete detachment. The best approach is to be friendly, sit down and talk respectfully to the tenant, and try to resolve the problem they have in paying their rent or their behaviour. However, if that's not possible, ask them to leave and do not get emotional. If you lose your temper (as I have often done) it is counterproductive. The conversation I have with my tenants goes along the lines of:

Me: "Mr Tenant, you are having difficulty in paying the rent you owe. I am very sorry but I cannot afford to allow this to continue so I am going to have to ask you to leave. When can you leave?"

Tenant: "I don't know. I will have to find somewhere else to live!"

Me: "Yes, you understand I am not asking you to leave today. How long do you think it will take to find somewhere else to live?"

Tenant: "About a week."

Me: "Ok, as long as you have gone by next week, I will forget what you owe me. Is that ok?"

(Note: The chance of recovering rent from unemployed tenants or blue collar workers who do not have regular employment, is almost nil. So you are not giving much away but it creates goodwill and motivates the tenant).

Tenant: "Yes, thanks very much."

Me: "Please don't forget to let me have the keys back. I will pop round during the week to see how things are going. Please let me know if you need any help in moving."

In most cases, it's that easy. I find that being nice works well. The tenant leaves on good terms and the problem is solved. Sometimes, I resort to giving a financial inducement and have provided transport, but generally I will leave the tenant to get on with it. When I later check the property, the tenant has gone. Occasionally, the tenant takes more time than they say they will to leave. In such cases, I try to keep it good-humoured and persist and the tenant usually leaves. This is not always the case though so you will have to use the court route to evict. I accept it is easier to get a bedsit tenant to leave than a family who has built up local ties. Bedsit tenants on the whole tend to be more nomadic.

I find it hard to be pleasant to a tenant who I know is conning me. They have had the rent money but would rather spend it on other things, usually alcohol and/or drugs and will have given me a whole load of lies and broken promises which I am gullible enough to believe. In my experience, it is rarely *'can't pay'*. In most cases, it is *'won't pay!'* This is where being able to detach yourself from the situation is essential. Even though you are aware that the tenant is conning you, pointing this out is not normally going to help you achieve your objective of getting the tenant to leave quickly and without any comebacks.

Your council may not like you asking your tenants to leave but it is all perfectly legal, providing it does not amount to harassment which would only be the case if you continually ask a tenant to leave. Some councils and tenancy support bodies are very anti-landlord and will go out of their way to encourage tenants to stay. They will even go so far as to tell them they do not have to move until a court order is obtained and the bailiffs evict them. Furthermore, there is nothing else the landlord can do if they do not pay any rent. Most councils are in competition with private landlords in that they also provide housing, yet they are not constrained by the same rules as private landlords when it comes to evicting tenants in HMOs and hostels. They can evict and do evict at will. I know this all sounds very paranoid but I can assure you from experience it happens more than you think. Yes, councils should be encouraging the private sector as there is an enormous shortage of housing but they are not the ones who are homeless. They see their role as the main provider of housing under attack. You need to remember that after World War II, the Labour Government nearly destroyed the private sector with rent controls and draconian legislation.

The private sector went from 90% to less than 10% of the population after World War II. At the same time, councils created enormous ghettos called council housing estates.

After 30 years, some are being demolished. The heavy costs to the taxpayer in paying for social housing doesn't seem to be affecting their decisions.

It does not help that other private landlords or landlord associations do not do much against the inequalities of the current law. I hope that with the rapid expansion of the private sector, this may bring forward more landlords who are prepared to fight against this injustice, but see little evidence. The tenants from hell I evict seem to have few problems in finding alternative accommodation from landlords who just do not seem to care they have been evicted. As I keep saying, there is little consequence to a tenant who causes trouble or refuses to pay their rent, apart from the fact that they will not be housed by me, one of the very best landlords in the area. However, this does not seem to worry them.

This behaviour is like a nature programme I once watched about rabbits. When a fox appears, only the rabbit that the fox is chasing runs away. The rest of the rabbits go on about their business. They instinctively know which one the fox is after and carry on eating, probably thinking, *'good, there is more grass for me now'*. They do not group together and in massed ranks attack the fox – even though with weight of numbers, they could beat the fox to death. There is no concept of 'next time'. There is no idea that, 'if we do not organise, the next target could be me!'

Surrender

The method that I have described about asking a tenant to leave is known as surrender. In practice, it works and there are rarely any comebacks. However, legally it is not as simple as I have made it appear. How a landlord proves the tenant has surrendered their tenancy is fraught with difficulties. The classic answer is that the tenant says they are leaving and hands back the keys to the property. From a landlord's point of view, it is safer if the tenant puts it in writing and signs a letter or note to this effect. This prevents the tenant from later claiming that they had temporarily handed the keys over so the landlord could do some repairs or for safekeeping. See the case of Odera v Ilqbal 2010 for what can happen if you get this wrong.

However, what happens if the tenant says they have left or are leaving but does not return the keys? Or, as I find is the norm, the tenant moves out of the property but leaves behind a considerable amount of possessions. In such circumstances, the only safe answer is to apply for a possession order in the court which can take nine weeks using my method (see www.hmodaddy.com). Many local authorities and social landlords do just that. They board up the property and wait.

They are not prepared to take the risk of being found guilty of illegal or unlawful eviction. Of course, they are funded by the taxpayers so the loss of rent is not quite the same thing to them.

Many new and often established landlords do not appreciate that the law takes very little account of whether the tenant is or is not paying the rent, is not occupying the property, has removed most of their belongings, or has very few possessions in the property. Tenants have been known to say in such circumstances that they were staying with a sick relative, took their possessions for safekeeping, or even say the landlord must have taken them.

I agree that the non-payment of rent is a matter that most landlords would consider of fundamental importance. I very much doubt any private sector landlord would care whether or not the tenant uses a property so long as they are paying the rent. The landlord is concerned when the tenant is not paying rent and does not appear to be living at the property.

Abandonment

In other words, the courts as a whole ignore the payment of rent – the issue is whether the tenant is in occupation or intends to return to the property. Serving an abandonment notice is thought to provide protection, but the law surrounding abandonment is unclear. It is not officially recognised by the courts but if correctly carried out, offers some protection against accusations of illegal eviction and harassment (the criminal charges) and may mitigate any civil action for harassment and unlawful eviction.

The usual advice regarding abandonment is that the landlord should take all reasonable steps to investigate what has happened to the tenant. Then they should do everything possible to try and contact the tenant and serve a notice on the property, giving about 14 days' notice. Then if the tenant does not contact him, the landlord may treat the tenant as having left.

The payment or non-payment of rent is irrelevant to this process. Direct payment of Housing Benefits is another matter because Housing Benefits can, in certain circumstances, be reclaimed from the landlord if the tenant was not living in the property.

The problem with abandonment is that it is not clear what the landlord should do and in what circumstances he should act. It is only proof of them acting decently. Following an abandonment procedure is not conclusive evidence that the tenant has left. Apart from the moral aspect of the landlord being seen doing all they can, the procedure will mainly be relevant in protecting the landlord against criminal charges of harassment and illegal eviction and may mitigate matters with unlawful eviction, the civil matter.

What should a landlord do if they have changed the locks and the tenant returns after appearing to have abandoned the property and says they have not left? If the landlord allows the tenant back into the property (assuming they have not rented the property to another party), then in practice that would solve the problem. So why bother in the first place with abandonment or even court eviction. Why not just change the locks and see what happens?

I am not suggesting that the answer is to forget abandonment, express surrender and court eviction. But if just letting the tenant return to the property, an alternative property, or paying them off solves the legal problem, then why be unduly concerned? If a tenant shows they care little about their obligations as a tenant by not paying the rent and appears to have left, you can understand the landlord not showing any greater concern about the tenant, in spite of the legalities.

Understand that the changing of locks or even doing less than that could be considered harassment, which is a criminal offence. If you immediately let the tenant return, it could still be construed as illegal or unlawful eviction but I think that scenario is unlikely, especially if the tenant has not had to find temporary alternative accommodation. However, this does not take into account the elaborate story that a clever, malicious or rapacious tenant who knows their rights could concoct out of the situation with the help of legal counsel.

Nearly all of the cases in this book relating to illegal and unlawful eviction have a common theme: the tenant has clearly indicated to the landlord that they do not want to leave or have not left. Usually, a solicitor or the local authority has intervened and asked the landlord to stop behaving as they are, doing, and/or to let the tenant return to the property. Yet, the landlord has ignored this legal intervention and has persisted in refusing to let the tenant return or even physically thrown the tenant out. In some cases, the landlord has continued in their course of action even after an injunction has been served on them. An injunction is a court order to refrain from a course of action or to do something. Failure to obey can result in unlimited fines and/or imprisonment.

These are not minor misunderstandings as to whether the tenant has left. They are continuous, blatant and deliberate courses of action on the landlord's part which have resulted in court action.

When the landlord is either entirely ignorant of the rights of a tenant or does not care, the landlord is of the erroneous belief that if they have told or asked the tenant to leave or if the tenant is not paying rent, then they should not have any entitlement to live at the property. As I explained earlier, this is not legally relevant. However, it will be of some comfort to landlords to know that nearly all of the cases on harassment, illegal or unlawful eviction that I have heard about that have gone to court all involve either a long period of continuous and sustained action by the landlord or this has continued after the intervention by the authorities or a solicitor.

There appears to be a considerable gap between what the law says is harassment, illegal and unlawful eviction and when legal action is taken. There are clear red lights flashing. For example, the landlord has continued to evict the tenant, in spite of being repeatedly warned by a solicitor or the council. In such circumstances, the landlord has only themselves to blame.

One landlord told me, "I just change the locks on problem

tenants and if they go to the Citizens' Advice Bureau or council, I let them back in. I have not had any problems with this approach so far!"

I have spoken to Tenancy Support Officers from the council and they all say the same thing. If the landlord stops harassing the tenant and lets the tenant return to the property, they do not take action. However, the council will often give the landlord a firm telling off. I should emphasise that this is not the law and I am in no way advocating that you do this or that the same will happen with you. I am only relating what happens in real life to reduce any paranoia surrounding this. As the following cases show, a tenant has to be genuinely and brutally evicted to be successful in claiming for unlawful eviction.

If asking does not work then I resort to the legal process of eviction, which involves:

Eviction through the Court

This is the only sure way to evict a tenant. Relying on surrender (unless in writing) or abandonment has flaws – though surrender and abandonment are how the vast majority of tenancies come to an end.

The process for eviction is contained in the Housing Act 1988, which states that you can only evict a tenant by court order using two routes:

A. Following the Section 21 route by giving two months' notice to vacate (NB. you cannot start the eviction process until the end of the fixed period of the tenancy or six months whichever is more, this is why most tenancies are for six months) for which no reason is needed or needs to be given, or

B. Following the Section 8 route, which has to be for one or more of the 17 reasons available to evict a tenant, though in practice it is always for rent arrears, known as Ground 8 (eight weeks' arrears) or Ground 10, any rent arrears.

The procedure is unnecessarily complicated and the court can be unsympathetic to the landlord who, in order to avoid the high cost of legal help, acts in person. It's also important to appreciate that most judges are pro-tenant and anti-landlord. It is also the responsibility of the landlord to clearly prove their case. For example, a landlord must prove that the tenant has arrears (a rent statement is usually considered sufficient) and the proper notices have been served and received by the tenant. The only good part is that most judges do not seem to know very much about the eviction process, so they rarely challenge what you do.

The cost of evicting a tenant is comprised of only the cost of the court summons if you do it yourself (which has gone up to £285, or costs £250 if done online) and invariably the lost rent while you wait for the court hearing which takes, depending on whether you do it online or not, 5 to 10 weeks. When giving a possession order, the court always allows the tenant at least 14 additional days to leave.

Then if they don't leave, it can take anywhere from another 14 to 100 days to get the bailiffs to act (period dependent on the bailiff's availability) at a further cost of £110. Sometimes it is much more cost-effective to use the High Court bailiffs to evict. Even though they cost 10 times more, they will act within seven days.

What I find surprising is that even for antisocial tenants, the courts take the same amount of time to grant an eviction. I have been faced with drug-dealing pimps running a brothel in my house who have refused to leave and I have had to go through the whole slow process. These tenants were in an HMO (a shared house) and either had other tenants dealing drugs for them or they had left. In such circumstances, I was unable to put new tenants into the property.

Luckily, once the drug-dealing pimps had been served with a court hearing, they became agreeable to a financial inducement to leave and left. Otherwise, it could have taken months to get rid of them. However, I had to ask the remaining tenants to leave, which they did without much trouble since they were all now involved in drug dealing and I closed the property for a few weeks until the nocturnal visits from other drug dealers and customers stopped. Why tenants involved in such damaging, illegal and antisocial behaviour are still required to be evicted by an expensive slow bureaucratic process defies any sense of justice or reason.

A few years ago, all you needed to do was issue a Section 21 or Section 8 notice and the tenant would leave within a few weeks. Now, nearly all tenants I evict using the courts, stay until the expiry of the possession order and increasingly more are now waiting for the bailiff. With there being no consequences for refusing to leave until the bailiff arrives, who can blame the tenants? It is the system that needs changing but there is little chance of that happening.

The sad fact is that landlords are considered as second-class citizens with no rights, derided by the social sector who see landlords as a major threat to their opulent taxpayer-funded lifestyle. They are also hounded by Council Housing Standards and Planning Enforcement Officers who have to justify their existence with little evidence that what they do is of any benefit to tenants or society.

If the feedback I get from my defaulting tenants is to be believed (which I do), Legal Advice Centres and Council Housing Departments appear to be encouraging tenants to stay until the bailiffs arrive. The Council Housing Departments even appear to be misleading tenants who go to them to be re-housed by telling the tenant that the council cannot re-house them until there is a possession order. Only when the tenant turns up with the possession order will the council look at the case and ask why the landlord has obtained a possession order. Usually when it's discovered that the order is for rent arrears or anti-social behaviour, the council says that the tenant has made themselves intentionally homeless and refuses to re-house them. Or, if the tenant is vulnerable, they will only be given temporary accommodation in hostels. The tenant is then left high and dry, in massive arrears of rent, because they were told by some *'well meaning'* council official that they don't have to pay the rent or that the landlord cannot do anything if they do not pay the rent!

Once realising that they will not be re-housed, some tenants will try to resolve the situation with their landlord. Usually the rent money has been squandered so they have massive arrears. I question why the council does not tell the tenants to sort out their rent arrears. I could continue about the council policy on handling bad or non-paying tenants but maybe we should save that for another book. To get back on topic, the court eviction procedure is not that difficult once you understand how to use it. However, it is very slow and totally unsympathetic to the landlord, but it is the only safe way to evict a tenant.

Conclusion

In comparison with much of the business of being a landlord, especially an HMO landlord (a landlord who multi lets, also known as houses in multiple occupation), when you try to follow *'the rules'* or the safe way you will not get very far. As a landlord, there is no fine line to walk. It is a very murky line you have to follow if you are to remain in business.

HMO Daddy has written a manual on how to evict tenants, and also runs courses (see www.hmodaddy.com).

Summary of Cases

Case	Date	Special (quantifiable)	General (unquantifiable)		
			Day rate	Total day rate	Other (e.g harassment etc.)
Deelah	2011		250	1,000	1,500
Evans	2009		250	15,750	
Salah	2009	1,000	200	8,600	
Schuchard	2010		200	24,000	
			125	4,975	
			26	2,000	
Walsh	2010	5,750	200	6,000	2,000
Anslow	2009		96	7,000	
Ogle	2009	1,054	167	2,171	
			334	2,338	
Lord	1999	420			1,000
		430			1,000
Murray	2008				
Fakhari	2010	2,995			2,000
Abbas	2009	5,494	250	750	1,000
Hunt	2009	100	125	8,125	45,000
Arabhalvaei	2008	2,601			46,500
		2,325			67,500
Naveed	2007	2,000			10,000
Odera	2010	750			1,000
Keddy	2010		165	4,620	1,500

Aggravated	Exemplary	Nominal	Disrepair	Interest	Total
(e.g. humiliation & distress)	(cost of eviction)	(e.g. trespass)			
1,500	2,500				6,500
1,000	2,000			1446.56	25,196
2,000	2,000				12,850
4,975	1,750				32,725
4,000	1,500			204	19,454
2,000	1,000			+ interest	10,000
2,300	1,400			+ interest	8,209
2,000	2,000			647	6067
1,000	2,000			518	5948
			9,000	225	9,225
	2,000		9,250		16,250
10,000	7,500		14,450		39,194
				3,453	65,678
5,000	500		24,825	37,099	184,026
15,000	Including aggravated				27,000
1,500	1,000	500			4,750
1,000	2,000				9,120

Cases on Illegal Eviction

1. The following cases illustrate the compensation that can be awarded to tenants for unlawful eviction.

2. I have deliberately chosen cases involving HMOs since I want to emphasise that the law applies to HMOs. Many of the cases have the similar features like the fact that a local authority Tenancy Relations Officer or a solicitor was involved and the landlords involved ignored them. I believe the amount of compensation awarded is disproportionate to the loss suffered by the tenant and it seems to me to show a degree of bias on behalf of judges to landlords. These types of exemplary and aggravated damages are rarely seen in other areas of law.

3. With most of these cases, it is clear that the tenants have profited massively from being evicted.

4. I suspect it has not cost the tenant a penny to bring these cases since they will have been Legally Aided. On the other hand, the defendants (i.e. the landlord) will have to pay for their defence and if they win would not be able to recover their costs because the Legal Aid Fund does not pay if it loses. The tenants would not be worth suing to recover the costs. Nowadays, tenants can use 'No Win No Fee' solicitors who can insure their costs which make things worse as solicitors are allowed to double their costs if they win.

5. Cases where a landlord wins are rarely reported because the bodies who report these cases are usually motivated towards supporting tenants and are anti-landlord. They wish to portray landlords in a bad light. Sometimes tenants and their lawyers can be scheming manipulators but this is rarely put into the public domain.

Deelah v Rehman: 2011

Clerkenwell and Shoreditch County Court

A remarkably small award of £6,500, given the circumstances

Mr. Deelah was an assured shorthold tenant in a shared two-storey flat above a shop (i.e. an HMO from February 2009). He had exclusive possession of one bedroom with shared use of a kitchen and bathroom. He lived there with his wife and two sons aged 9 and 16. His landlord, Mr. Rehman, ran a mobile phone shop below. There were two other bedrooms in the flat. One of these was occupied by a friend of the landlord, Mr. Zuhai, and the other by a couple of Mr. Zuhai's relatives.

In June 2010, Mr. Rehman asked Mr. Deelah to take a tenancy of the whole flat. After he refused, Mr. Rehman told him to leave, saying he had agreed to re-let the flat to Mr. Zuhai's relative. On 22nd June, Mr. Rehman came to Mr. Deelah's room with a neighbouring shopkeeper. The shopkeeper accused Mr. Deelah of using his commercial wastebin and behaved aggressively. Later that day, Mr. Rehman seized Mr. Deelah's forearm during a further row and twisted it. He threatened to change the locks and throw the family's belongings into the street. On 20th July, Mr. Deelah returned with his 16-year-old son to find the locks had been changed. The son climbed over a fence to try and gain access. The landlord swore at him and threatened to kill him, approaching him with an iron bar.

The family was ineligible for homelessness assistance. They had to stay with a friend, sleeping on a sofa and the floor in the friend's living room. The children missed school. Mr. Deelah obtained an injunction. Mr. Rehman initially refused to re-admit them, suggesting he had already re-let the flat. However, he later complied with the injunction. The family moved back in and recovered their belongings. Mr. Rehman sought to defend the claim on the basis that Mr. Zuhai, not he, was the landlord. His defence was later struck out for failure to comply with directions (directions are instructed from the court as to what evidence is required). He failed to attend the final hearing.

There was evidence of further harassment after the injunction, including two occasions when Mr. Deelah had been unable to get into or out of his room for short periods because the lock had been tampered with.

The judge extended the injunction and awarded damages as follows:

- £1,000 for the four nights during which the family had been excluded (£250 per night).

- £1,500 for the harassment before and after the eviction.

- £1,500 aggravated damages.

- £2,500 exemplary damages, on the basis that the eviction had been intended to save the landlord the cost of court proceedings. The evidence suggested the property was probably an unlicensed HMO. The judge accepted that the costs of recovering possession lawfully were likely to be more expensive as a result.

Total award of £6,500.

COMMENT

If all cases on unlawful eviction were like this, I would suggest that landlords have little to worry about since:

Firstly, it was a clear-cut case of harassment and unlawful eviction and the landlord had been adequately warned by being serviced with an injunction. This is not a case where the landlord is unsure whether the tenant had left or not, and he was clearly in the wrong.

Secondly, the award was for only £6,500 though the legal costs will have been a lot more. We know nothing about the tenant's circumstances. I would suggest that awarding £250 for the four nights the family of four were homeless was modest. To give £250 a night for a single male is rather different:

Evans Ozkan v Hussein 2009, where £250 a night for 63 nights was awarded.

Salah v Munro 2009, where £200 per night for 43 nights was awarded.

Schuchard v Fu 2010, where £200 per night for 43 nights was awarded.

Walsh v Shuangyan 2010 were given £200 per night for 30 nights.

Ogle v Bundhoo 2009 were awarded £334 per night for 7 nights.

Giving only £1,500 for harassment and £1,500 for aggravated damages seems modest in the circumstances.

In Abbas v Iqbal 2009, aggravated damages of £10,000 was awarded.

In Naveed v Raja 2007, aggravated damages of £15,000 was awarded.

Deelah v Reham is a later case than the other two cases so it may show a more conservative approach to awarding compensation.

The problem with cases like these is that you are often left with many unanswered questions such as, why was Deelah ineligible for homeless assistance? They were clearly overcrowded, the four of them living in one room. Also, was Deelah paying rent or was he in arrears?

The landlord did not help himself in showing contempt and deviousness in not attending the later hearings, being slow to comply with the injunction, and trying to pretend he was not the landlord. This kind of behaviour brings all landlords into disrepute.

Evans Ozkan v Hussein: 2009

Legal Action 33 – 2009 Luton County Court

Damages of £250 per day after eviction for HMO tenant with a total award of £25,196

Mr Evans was an assured shorthold tenant of a room at a weekly rental of £100. Before signing the tenancy agreement and handing over the deposit of £400, he told his landlord that he was receiving income support and would need to claim Housing Benefit. About a month later, delays in payment led to an intimidating visit by Mr, Hussein, the landlord, who demanded £1,000 which Mr Evans did not have.

On 21st March 2007, Mr. Evans returned home to find some of his belongings on the pavement. The defendant and two other men were throwing out more of his things. Mr. Hussein was verbally intimidating. The police became involved and Mr. Evans was arrested. On his release that evening, he found many of his belongings lying on the pavement, crushed or smashed. The lilo he had been using as a mattress was deflated and full of holes. Other possessions were missing. Furthermore, his ruined belongings smelled of urine.

Mr. Evans spent the night in his car, but returned the next day to find that the locks had been changed. The defendants followed Mr. Evans to the local pub, threatened him with baseball bats and demanded £1,000, making it clear that he would not get his belongings back until he had paid. Further threats were made. Mr. Evans applied to the council for homelessness assistance and was re-housed. In the intervening period, he spent 63 nights without a home and his health deteriorated. He also suffered from thoughts of suicide. Mr. Evans claimed damages for trespass, harassment and unlawful eviction.

The judge awarded:

- £15,750 general damages (£250 per day for the whole period that Mr. Evans was homeless) and interest of £883.73 for the period from the day he was re-housed to the date of the hearing.

- £5,000 special damages.

- £1,000 aggravated damages.

- £2,000 exemplary damages and £562.85 interest for the period from the date of the eviction to the date of the hearing.

The judge considered the damages that would otherwise have been payable under the Protection from Harassment Act 1997 formed part of the award in aggravated damages. Exemplary damages were awarded because the defendant had sought to avoid the due process of law, that is the eviction process and the costs attended on that.

A total award of £25,196.

COMMENT

This is what I call a jackpot case. To many unemployed single people, this is a fantastic result. To someone who is only getting £70 pw on benefit to be awarded almost 8 years' income, tax free, is beyond their dreams. I would suspect most of my readers earn in excess of £30,000 pa, so imagine being awarded £250,000, tax free, for the same thing. Yes, I accept it is unpleasant to be homeless but not the worst thing to happen to you and totally disproportionate to other awards.

This case involved a room in a house occupied for only four weeks at a rent of £100 per week. It was hardly a home where you could be said to have deprived a tenant of a settled existence. I would have a different view if the tenant had been a family settled in the property.

I am not in any way condoning the appalling behaviour of the landlord, Hussein, or the strange behaviour of the police in arresting Evans. Perhaps Evans should also consider suing the police. He was probably getting Legal Aid so it would cost him nothing; the solicitors would do it all for him.

I wonder what evidence was produced as to the threats of baseball bats or his possessions being smashed and smelling of urine. Moreover, Hussain was lucky that the judge did not appear to award anything for the deterioration in mental health; see case of Hunt v Hussain where £45,000 was awarded. The judge only awarded £1,000 in aggravated damages, which seems very low given the circumstances compared to other cases. See my comments on the previous case where aggravated damages of up to £15,000 have been awarded for similar treatment. I also ask why it took 63 days to re-house Evans. Surely this could have been done more quickly? I believe there are questions about the time it is alleged it takes to re-house many of the tenants who have been unlawfully evicted.

Salah v Munro: 2009

July 2009 Legal Action 31 Willesden County Court

A case which clearly illustrates that using the eviction process is cheaper! An award of £12,850.

Ms. Salah occupied a room in a house as an assured shorthold tenant at a rent of £700 per month. Her tenancy commenced on 23rd March 2008 and was for a fixed term of six months. She was granted Housing Benefit which was, even after appeal, less than the full rent. Her landlord had a policy of not accepting Housing Benefit claimants as tenants. On discovering Ms. Salah's Housing Benefit claim, he told her to leave and said that he would return to throw her out.

On 25th May 2008, the landlord, his brother, and his girlfriend attended and demanded that Ms. Salah leave and return her keys. She refused, but left the property temporarily taking the key with her. On her return, she found that the locks had been changed and her belongings missing. She spent one night in a hospital following an asthma attack, two nights in bed and breakfast accommodation, and eight nights on a sofa in a friend's flat before being readmitted following a court order. Following the readmission, the landlord continued to harass Ms. Salah, including falsely accusing her of being a prostitute. Some of the room furniture had been removed and was not replaced.

Following the expiry of the fixed term tenancy, the landlord disabled the electricity and gas forcing Ms. Salah to sleep at a friend's property from 3rd October 2008 to 7th November

2008. The electricity was reconnected one month after a request was made by Ms. Salah's solicitor and only on the landlord being notified that Legal Aid had been extended to cover a committal application. A committal application is an application to have the landlord sent to prison for failing to comply with the injunction. Thereafter, Ms. Salah slept at the property only intermittently and otherwise continued to stay with her friend. On 3rd January 2009, the landlord called the police to the property when he saw Ms. Salah there. The police confiscated her keys.

The judge awarded:

- £8,600 general damages in respect of unlawful eviction for the 43 nights she was excluded from the property, on the basis that the usual range was between £100 to £300 per night, and the appropriate level in the case was £200.

- £2,000 aggravated damages.

- £2,000 exemplary damages.

- £1,000 special damages, conservatively estimated in the absence of any receipts.

From the award, the judge deducted arrears of rent amounting to £750 having excluded totally the periods of Ms. Salah's exclusion and abating by half the rent for the period when Ms. Salah was deprived of gas.

A total award of £12,850.

COMMENT

Here, we have a tenant who possibly misrepresented herself as a working tenant when she was a benefit tenant (a tenant whose rent is paid by Housing Benefit). What's worse is that she evidently took on a property that she could not afford, even when obtaining full Housing Benefit. The report says that the landlord would not take Housing Benefit tenants. The above does not allow the landlord to physically remove a tenant and even more stupidly, the landlord continued to harass his tenant after a court order had been obtained. Why the landlord did not evict the tenant for rent arrears as Grounds 8 and 10 (which gives the landlord the ability to evict for this reason at any time) instead of waiting until the expiry of her fixed term of six months seems odd. He may have also been able to evict for obtaining accommodation by misrepresentation, Ground 17.

As for the procedure to evict tenants, see my manual *DIY Eviction* available only from my website www. hmodaddy.com.

Then the landlord tried to harass the tenant again and was assisted by the police, who took the keys of the tenant. This is very strange behaviour and I wonder if she also sued them?

A compensation award of £12,850, considering the landlord had received an injunction and had warnings from a solicitor, was not disproportionate when taking into account the landlord's outrageous behaviour to his tenant. I feel the judge was also more than fair in allowing a deduction of £750 for rent arrears.

Schuchard v Fu: 2010

Brentford County Court

Legal Action 36, 25th February 2010

This case illustrates how much an evicted tenant can be awarded if alternative accommodation is not found. He was awarded £32,725!

In this HMO room case, Mr. Schuchard was the tenant. The landlord wanted him out so she could do renovation work. She sent a letter but no Section 21 notice. The property was situated in Brentford, London.

On 6th July, Fu wrote asking Schuchard to leave the next day because of rent arrears. On 7th July, she changed the lock to the front door and refused to give him the new key. The following day, the local council's Tenancy Relationship Officer (TRO) asked her to readmit Mr. Schuchard but she refused, saying that she would only let him in again if the rent arrears were paid. She continued to refuse to allow him in when his solicitor wrote to her.

Mr. Schuchard was homeless for 120 days because he, his solicitor, and the TRO were unable to find him accommodation. He was then housed for 77 days by the local authority, but after that he spent the next 35 days up to the trial sleeping on a friend's floor.

The judge awarded:

- £24,000 general and aggravated damages at £200 per day for the 120 days he was homeless or on the street.

- £2,000 for the 77 days he was given accommodation by the local authority at a rate of £26 per day.

- £4,975 general and aggravated damages at a daily rate of £125 for 35 days for the final period when he was living on a friend's floor.

- £1,750 exemplary damages, as the landlord had evicted him so she could do up the property and for disregarding his rights.

A total award of £32,725.

COMMENT

I find it strange that the Local Council Tenancy Relationship Officer or Schudard's solicitor did not apply for an injunction, but just tried to find the tenant, Mr. Suchard, other accommodation and then only for 35 days. The amount of the award, as I have pointed out before, is totally disproportionate to the loss or harm suffered. I even fail to see the justification for the £25 per night for the 11 weeks he was housed by the local authority. I can evict a tenant legally within nine weeks, yet to allow compensation to run on for over 33 weeks seems bizarre.

This case also illustrates the unfair position between local authorities and private sector landlords in that local authorities can evict hostel residents at will, yet private sector landlords have to use the court process.

In the case of Hunt v Hussain: 2009, the judge at least limited the time to what it would have taken to have evicted the tenant. Hunt's case is the only case I know where this has happened.

You cannot tell (from the cases) how long it would have taken to find alternative accommodation. I do not know the situation with Brentford, a suburb of London, but in my area the Tenancy Relationship Officer tells me they can accommodate single people who do not have issues (e.g. alcoholics, drug addicts) within 48 hours. Whether the time it should take to find accommodation was argued in this case, I do not know, but it should have been because there is normally a duty to the claimant in a case to mitigate (reduce) their loss.

Walsh v Shuangyan: 2010

June 2010: Legal Action 35, Manchester County Court

A landlady was sent to prison for 28 days for breaking an injunction and the tenant received £20,000 for unlawful (civil) eviction.

This concerned a tenancy for a room in an HMO. The local authority served notices on the landlady as she failed to obtain an HMO licence and do various remedial works. As a result of the boiler and electricity being disconnected, all the tenants except Mr. Walsh moved out.

Mr. Walsh was then subjected to a reign of harassment and intimidation by the landlord and her father, who also assaulted him. On one occasion, he had to barricade himself into his room while they were in the house.

On 16th September, he arrived home to find the locks had been changed and some of his possessions put into bags. The rest of his possessions were still inside the room where he could not get to them. He complained to the local authority's Tenancy Relations Officer (TRO) who spoke to the landlady but she still refused to let him return to the property. She also refused to comply with an injunction obtained by Mr. Walsh and was committed to prison for 28 days. Mr. Walsh had to sleep on friends' sofas for 30 days, missed work, and developed a painful back.

The judge awarded:

- £2,000 for harassment before the eviction.

- £6,000 for the eviction and its consequences (based on a 'daily rate' of £200).

- £4,000 for aggravated damages.

- £1,500 exemplary damages (representing the costs the landlord might have incurred had she sought advice and evicted Mr. Walsh lawfully).

- £5,750 special damages for his lost possessions and earnings.

- £204 interest.

- Costs on an indemnity basis.

Total £19,454 (plus the indemnity costs).

COMMENT

This case is a good example of the power of an injunction, though to be sent to prison for 28 days for breach thereof seems very draconian given the circumstances. Very few breaches of injunctions result in imprisonment and I fail to see the benefit to anyone in sending the landlady to prison, especially since she also had to pay £19,454 of which £4,000 is for aggravated damages designed to punish the landlady, which seems like a high amount.

People get sent to prison for criminal offences, however, the civil courts have power to imprison a person in very limited circumstances, one being for breaking an injunction. The person is treated as a civil prisoner, which means that even though they are within the normal prison system they have a few rights which criminal prisoners do not have. Usually it is very hard to get sent to prison for a criminal offence and very few women are sent to prison. It is generally not realised that less than 2% of the prisoner population are women, as television shows a lot of programmes depicting women in prison. Equal opportunities have not reached the criminal justice system. This landlady would have to work very hard to have been sent to prison as a criminal. It shows how extreme the law is against landlords.

Overall, I believe this to be a completely disproportionate punishment for the landlady and an excessively high award for the tenant. When I was an HMO tenant, I would have happily slept on a friend's sofa for far less than £200 per night. I often did this, but did not get paid.

Anslow v Hayes: 2009

15th October 2009, Manchester County Court

A low daily rate of only £96

In this HMO room case, the tenant, Mr. Anslow accrued some arrears and as a result was threatened with eviction by his landlord. He arrived home to find he was not allowed to enter. He contacted Mr. Hayes to get him allowed back in, but Mr. Hayes refused and insisted on reporting him to the police.

Mr. Anslow got help from the council's Tenancy Relationship Officer (TRO) and a solicitor, but he was still refused admittance. His girlfriend had to go in to get his possessions, but some were never recovered including some items of high sentimental value, which were disposed of or removed without his consent. He spent 73 days in cramped conditions with his girlfriend before finding somewhere else to live.

The judge awarded:

- £7,000 general damages to compensate him for the 73 days that he was deprived of his home – a daily rate of only £96.

- £2,000 aggravated damages, taking into account the fact that Hayes had been warned that his conduct was illegal.

- £1,000 exemplary damages (representing the costs the landlord might have incurred had he sought advice and evicted Mr. Anslow lawfully).

- Interest and costs.

A total award of £10,000 plus costs.

COMMENT

A comparatively moderate award given the circumstances. It seems totally out of line with other awards. Maybe the tenant having to live with his girlfriend in *'cramped conditions'* was not considered as bad as living on a *'friends'* floor or sofa!

I find it odd that it took over 10 weeks to find alternative HMO accommodation in Manchester. It doesn't normally take that long and unfortunately, you cannot tell if it was challenged from the report. In Manchester, I am reliably informed that in 2009 you could find HMO accommodation within a day.

A special award for lost possessions seems to be missing, yet it was alleged that possessions were lost. The aggravated damages are in line with other cases, especially considering the landlord had been warned about his conduct was illegal. The exemplary damages were unusually low; most of the cases I have seen allow £2,000 not £1,000.

Ogle v Bundhoo: 2009

September 2009: Legal Action, Mayor's and City of London Court

Daily rate of £167 in B&B, and £334 for sleeping rough. A total of £8,209 + interest even though the tenant was allowed to return to the property

The claimant was the assured shorthold tenant of a bedsit. He shared a kitchen and bathroom with four other residents. He had paid the defendant, his landlord, a rental deposit. The claimant fell into two months' arrears with his rent and was advised by his landlord, the defendant, that he wanted him to leave the premises. The defendant left a letter for the claimant stating that the tenancy had ceased. The claimant contacted the defendant and told him that he could clear the arrears, but the defendant said that he still wanted him to leave. The same day, the claimant, after visiting the Jobcentre, returned to find that the lock to the house had been changed and that he was unable to access his room or his belongings. The defendant refused to allow him to re-enter the premises though he did offer to allow the claimant to collect his belongings, which had been placed outside his room. Since the claimant was homeless, he had nowhere to store them.

The claimant went to Citizens' Advice Bureau (CAB) but the defendant would not speak to the CAB advisor. After spending 13 nights in a B&B hotel and seven nights sleeping rough, the claimant instructed solicitors who obtained a without notice injunction. On being served with the injunction, the defendant allowed the claimant back into the premises. In his defence, the defendant accepted liability for the cost of the B&B and for three times the rental deposit because it had not been placed with a rental deposit scheme. The day before trial, the defendant sought an adjournment in a faxed letter to the court. He had already been debarred from adducing evidence for his failure to comply with directions.

The judge refused the application for an adjournment.

The judge awarded:

- £4,509 for breach of covenant for quiet enjoyment and trespass at the rate of £167 per night for the nights that the claimant was in the B&B, and £334 per night for the nights that the claimant was sleeping rough.

- £1,054 special damages made up for the three times the rental deposit and the cost of the B&B.

- £2,300 aggravated damages.

- £1,400 exemplary damages.

He also awarded interest at the rate of 8 percent of the damages, extended the injunction for a further year and reserved any application to set aside judgement to himself. The defendant was ordered to pay for the claimant's costs.

A total award of £8,209 + interest.

COMMENT

It was lucky that the landlord followed the injunction because judging from the tone of the award given, I think the judge would have treated him very severely if he had not. The daily rate of £334 is the highest rate for sleeping rough I have come across, though it was for only seven nights and the daily rate of £167 for living in a B&B was also the highest I have seen (compared to the £96 per night awarded in Anslow v Hayes 2009 for having to live in cramped conditions with his girlfriend, and £26 a night in Schuchard v Fu: 2010 for being temporarily housed by the local authority).

Unsuccessful Use of a Licence

Lord and Haslewood–Orgam v Jessop: 1999

August 1999: Legal Action 28 Court Appeal

There were two claimants in this case and so, there were two separate awards. The claimants occupied separate bed-sitting rooms with shared use of a bathroom and toilet. They signed *'licence agreements'*, but His Honour Justice Milligan held that they had assured tenancies. Ms. Lord fell into arrears because of reduction in the amount of Housing Benefit she received. The landlord constantly threatened Ms. Lord with eviction, telephoned her almost daily, entered her room without permission, was aggressive and implied that there might be violence. He changed the locks and did not give her a key. These events culminated in a suicide attempt.

Ms. Haslewood-Ogram complained about a lack of heating, and while she was out the landlord changed the lock. Her possessions were either locked in the room or thrown out of the rear of the house, and she was left with only the clothes that she was wearing. She was extremely upset.

The judge described the landlord's behaviour as *'discourteous, insulting, humiliating, threatening and disgraceful, self-interested and bullying'*.

The judge awarded Ms. Lord damages of £6,067.82 comprising:

- £1,000 damages for breach of covenant for quiet enjoyment up to the eviction.

- £2,000 damages for unlawful eviction.

- £2,000 aggravated damages.

- £420 special damages.

- £647.82 interest.

A total award to Ms. Lord of £6067.82.

The judge awarded Ms. Haslewood-Orgam damages of £5,948.95 comprising:

- £1,000 damages for breach of covenant for quiet enjoyment up the eviction.

- £2,000 damages for unlawful eviction.

- £1,000 for aggravated damages.

- £430 special damages for unlawful eviction.

- £1,000 aggravated damages.

- £518-95 interest.

A total award to Ms Haselwood–Organ of £5,948-95.

COMMENT

This case involved two tenants in the same house who were evicted at the same time. The significance of whether it was a licence or an Assured Shorthold Tenancy (AST) escapes me since you cannot evict a residential occupier without a court order, no matter what the agreement is called*. Maybe if the use of a licence had been upheld, then I would have found out. There appears to have been no allegation of having to sleep rough in both of these cases, yet special damages were still awarded of £420 and £430 but no explanation given for what those damages were. Both tenants received £1,000 each for harassment up to the eviction, something only occasionally awarded in eviction cases.

The behaviour towards Ms. Lord was worse and the effect more severe given that she attempted suicide as a result. Yet she only received an extra £1,000 in aggravated damages than Ms. Haslewood-Organ. If you compare this to Hunt v Hussain: 2009 where £45,000 was awarded for psychiatric injury, it seems like a very small amount. It may go to show how far the recognition of psychiatric injury had advanced in the 10 years between the cases.

*For more information on the differences between licences and ASTs see Appendix 3.

Illegal Eviction (Criminal) and Unlawful Eviction (Civil)

Be aware that you can also be prosecuted for illegal eviction or harassment where you can receive a fine and even be imprisoned, though prosecutions for illegal eviction are rare. The fine is paid to the state. Illegal eviction is removing a tenant without a court order, which is the same as unlawful eviction. So you could ask why all the landlords who have been found liable for unlawful eviction were also not prosecuted. Harassment is widely drafted and means the same as its civil equivalent and is anything that interferes with a tenant's quiet enjoyment of the property. Asking a tenant to pay the rent could be construed as harassment if the tenant did not want you to. Normally, harassment must be more than a one-off action and is usually considered to be action such as: cutting off the utilities, continually calling or going into the property without permission. Locking out the tenant would also amount to harassment and illegal eviction.

Getting prosecuted does not prevent unlawful eviction. In fact, it will probably encourage it – or at least civil action for compensation. It is not generally realised that most criminal acts can also give rise to a civil action, but very rarely does this happen as the majority of criminals are not worth suing. The O. J. Simpson case is one of the most notorious exceptions in that the compensation was awarded for the death of his wife and it also illustrates the different standards of proof that are supposed to exist between civil and criminal cases. It's often quoted on the *'balance of probabilities'* in civil cases and *'beyond reasonable doubt'* in criminal cases. In other words, even if you are acquitted of a criminal offence you could still be found liable in civil law on the same evidence. Landlords are usually always worth suing since they own what is considered the most valuable asset an individual can own, property.

Asghar v Ahmed: 1985

17 HLR 25 Court of Appeal

This is not an HMO case. The tenant and his family were unlawfully evicted by their landlord, who threw all their belongings onto the street. Despite the tenant obtaining an injunction, the landlord delayed in readmitting them. The landlord was convicted under Protection from Eviction Act 1977, fined £750, and ordered to pay £250 costs. In the County Court, the judge awarded aggravated damages of £500 and exemplary damages of £1,000 in addition to special damages.

The landlord's appeal was dismissed. It was as *'plain a case for aggravated damages as one would expect to find'*. The court of appeal declined to overturn the award of exemplary damages even though the landlord had been fined in the Crown Court. There was a great deal more to the landlord's conduct that followed the eviction which justified the finding that this was an outrageous example of persecution by a landlord of a tenant.

COMMENT

This is not an HMO case and older than most of the cases commented on. It also illustrates that a landlord can be prosecuted for illegal eviction (criminal) and also have compensation awarded against the landlord in civil court. The courts treat each action separately so a landlord is in double jeopardy prosecuted by the state and sued by the tenant.

I do not think the landlord realised his luck in being fined so little (£750 plus £250 costs) when a term of imprisonment is often given. (See Oxford City Council v Kenston McIntosh 2010 where the landlord was sent to prison for three months and Sheffield City Council v Allen 2013 where the landlord was imprisoned for nine months.)

Distinguish being sent to prison for illegal eviction which is a criminal offence where a criminal record is given, and being sent to prison for breaching an injunction as in Walsh v Shuangyan 2010. Breaking an injunction can result in the offender being imprisoned for a civil matter where no criminal record arises. It is one of the very rare times a person can be imprisoned by a civil court and seems to be mainly reserved for landlords who unlawfully evict. It only goes to show how harshly landlords are treated.

The level of aggravated damages awarded (£500) by the court to Asghar v Anmed for unlawful eviction was also very low compared to current cases. Some examples include:

Deelah v Rehman: 2011 - £1,500

Schuchard v Fa: 2010 - £4,975

Arabhalvaei v Rezaeipoor: 2008 - £5,000

Abbas v Iqbal: 2009 - £10,000

Naveed v Raja: 2007 - £15,000

Oxford City Council v Kenston McIntosh: 2010

Landlord guilty of illegal eviction and jailed for three months

A landlord was jailed for three months for unlawfully evicting a tenant from his property. Mr. Kenston McIntosh pleaded guilty to unlawful eviction after a hearing at Oxford Crown Court. The court heard that Mr. McIntosh had accepted that he had evicted his tenant, Mr. Michael Hutchinson, without a court order but maintained that he had provided accommodation to him as an act of charity.

Oxford City Council became involved in the case when officers received a phone call from Mr. Hutchinson. He had been living at the property in Balfour Road since 2006 and paid rent in cash to his landlord. His circumstances changed when he stopped working and applied for Housing Benefit. The council told him that they could not process his claim without proof from the landlord that he was living at the property. Mr. McIntosh refused to provide this information and asked Mr. Hutchinson to leave the property.

Mr. Hutchinson sought advice from the Council's Tenancy Relations Officer who wrote to Mr. McIntosh, informing him of Mr. Hutchinson's rights to remain in the property. In response to that letter, Mr. McIntosh served an invalid notice on Mr. Hutchinson seeking possession.

On 27th March 2010, Mr. McIntosh attended the property and became aggressive, telling Mr. Hutchinson to leave the property and that the locks would be changed. Following the eviction, Mr. Hutchinson was forced to sleep in an abandoned car.

Mr. McIntosh was previously arrested at Gatwick Airport on 2nd October 2010 after he failed to attend an earlier court hearing while on unconditional bail. He was held in custody at Crawley Police Station over that weekend and then transferred to Oxford Magistrates Court on the Monday.

He was released on conditional bail to attend the hearing on Friday, 29th October 2010 at Oxford Crown Court.

Councillor Joe McManners, Board Member of Housing, said, "There is a clear legal process for landlords to follow should they wish to evict a tenant. Mr. McIntosh failed to follow that process in this case and has paid the price. The court has sent out a strong message that it is simply not acceptable to evict a tenant without a court order."

Mr. McIntosh was jailed for three months. No costs were awarded.

COMMENT

The Oxford case shows just how harsh the council and courts can be towards HMO landlords who provide a valuable and much-needed service. I would have a different view if this was a family home, not simply a room in a house. Jailing the landlord was totally disproportionate when you consider who is and who is not sentenced to imprisonment. Moreover, I believe Oxford City Council to be anti-landlord. They did not have to prosecute the landlord; it is at the council's discretion to prosecute, especially as the tenant would have adequate remedies in the civil courts for compensation. The landlord had asked the tenant to leave and gave him time to do so, but failed to follow the proper procedure. So what? Does this justify prosecuting the landlord? It is not as if the landlord had thrown the tenant onto the street without notice. The council's hypocrisy is amplified in that within their own hostels, they can evict at will without any court order. It seems to me that they can be much too severe when dealing with the private sector.

On the other hand, the landlord was stupid not to pay attention to the council and treated them with contempt. Oxford Council did warn him and I doubt that matters would have progressed to prosecution if he had paid attention to them. However, in regards to all around fairness, I would have preferred that the council had, as they are duty bound to do, done more to warn the landlord of the consequences of his actions and maybe even tried the civil route and issued an injunction first. Even though the landlord could not be bothered to turn up to court, I doubt the extra warnings would have had much effect.

I do not have all of the facts of the case, but based on the information given, I am not convinced the tenant was, by law, a tenant. He appeared to be a lodger. Asking a tenant to leave is not a crime and the evidence that the tenant was illegally evicted seems very flimsy. If the tenant had left after being asked to go, then you could argue that the tenant had surrendered their tenancy. If the landlord had bothered to enter a defence, I think he may have been acquitted.

Contrary to popular opinion, criminal prosecutions are not always fully thought out. The evidence can be flimsy and can be no more than the person bringing the prosecution on a whim. A robust defence would destroy such action. But more often than not, landlords are too trusting and believe that if the council says they are guilty, then they must be. Other times, they might even feel it would be cheaper to plead guilty than to defend.

I do not know why councillor Joe McManners was so keen to uphold what was such an obviously unfair, bureaucratic and lengthy eviction process. In this case, the tenant was not refusing to pay the rent – he couldn't as he had lost his job – but he was prepared to make a Housing Benefit application which would have ensured that Kenston Mcintosh was paid his rent in full for 13 weeks! All Mcintosh had to do was acknowledge that Hutchinson was a tenant and the rent was due. I am, as a landlord, very grateful of our benefits system which, though horrendously bureaucratic, pays the rent for unemployed tenants. I have found in over 20 years of experience as a landlord that there is no justification as to why a tenant cannot pay their rent. If the tenant cannot afford to do so, the state will provide the tenant with Housing Benefit. If the tenant has run up arrears, they can usually get a Discretionary Housing payment as well as help with paying the arrears.

Sheffield City Council v Allen: 2013

Landlord guilty of illegal eviction – jailed for nine months

A Sheffield landlord who threw a tenant onto the streets with no shoes when he accrued rent arrears has been convicted of unlawful eviction and sentenced to nine months' imprisonment.

Jay Allen, 30, evicted Chris Blades with the help of a friend after he ran up £900 of arrears on the rental property in Sheffield. He gave no notice and did not seek a possession order.

The judge at Sheffield Crown Court said that Allen had tried to dominate and frighten his tenant. Allen has previous convictions for assault.

- UK Landlord January/February 2013.

COMMENT

The article shows how harshly the courts can treat landlords who illegally evict tenants, even if the tenant was not paying the rent. Imagine a shopkeeper being sent to prison for evicting a shoplifter!

Rarely in my experience is it the case that a tenant cannot pay. When working, it seems that some of them choose to spend the money on other things and if they cannot afford to pay or are unemployed, they could claim Housing Benefit. If they claim Housing Benefit, they have had the money but some go on to use for things like drugs and alcohol. In other words, they stole it or could not be bothered to claim Housing Benefit. I am not saying this with reference to Jay Allen but am making general observations. I wonder what goes through the mind of the judges and the prosecuting authorities when applying such one-sided and unfair legislation.

I do not know why the lack of notice is mentioned since it would not have made any difference as an eviction can only be legally made by obtaining a possession order. If the tenant still remains in possession, the bailiffs should be used to remove the tenant.

Disrepair

It gets worse for landlords. If the tenant is claiming for unlawful eviction or even if defending an eviction claim, they can also claim for disrepair and the compensation can substantially increase. A tenant can make a claim for disrepair even if not being evicted, though the attempt to evict a tenant appears to trigger disrepair and other claims.

Murray v Kelly: 2008

Clerkenwell and Shoreditch County Court

Counterclaim for disrepair: £9,225 awarded

In a possession action, a tenant counterclaimed for an extended period of disrepair lasting over eight years. This cost a landlord £9,225 plus his court costs.

The tenant's counterclaim amounted to £10,395 and consisted of the following problems:

- Low shower pressure from August 1998 to February 2007.

- Lack of heating from January to March 2000.

- A leaking shower from May 2005 to February 2007.

- No hot water for three weeks in 2005.

- Leaking wash basin from late 2005 to early 2007.

- A washing machine leaking for two years.

The Judge acknowledged that the landlord had attempted to do the repairs but had not done them properly and awarded the tenant £9,000 in damages, plus £225 interest accruing for the period of the disrepair.

COMMENT

The level of compensation awarded in disrepair cases is unbelievable for minor faults which the tenant could have easily remedied themselves. Repairs can take time, especially if parts are required. It is a shame there is no breakdown of what was awarded for each of the six faults or what notice, if any, the landlord had of the faults as I suspect the court required little evidence that the landlord was aware of the faults or had been reminded.

In order to cover themselves against any claims for disrepair, a landlord should keep a log of faults with dates and times of the reported fault and when they were repaired. Whenever possible, get the tenant to sign a satisfaction notice that not only acknowledges that the fault has been repaired to the tenant's satisfaction, but also there are no other faults. This makes it less likely that the tenant can allege long-running repairs.

With my own letting, I give a log number to the tenant to prove they have reported the fault. I have found that some tenants lie about reporting repairs and will complain they reported a fault months or even years ago, but are vague on dates and can provide no names of who they reported the fault to. Understandably, the fault if it was reported has been forgotten or we assume it has been repaired as the tenant never followed it up. In my tenancy agreement, it is a requirement to report faults in writing to help prove whether or not the fault was reported. If a tenant does report a fault in writing, I always write back and ask the tenant if the repairs have been carried out to their satisfaction so I have evidence the work had been done. When possible, I also get a written form which the tenant signs to say the work has been done to their satisfaction.

I would guess that the cost of repairs for all six faults in Murray v Kelly would amount to less than £500. So why did the tenant not do the repairs and deduct the cost of the repairs from the rent? See the advice given by Shelter (reproduced) where it is *the duty of the tenant to take reasonable action themselves to reduce their loss. Tenants can, by law, in writing, give the landlord a reasonable time to do the repairs and state if the landlord does not do the repair they will do it themselves and charge the landlord.* I wonder why this was not argued in the case? All very anti-landlord!

Fakhari v Newman: 2010

June 2010: Legal Action 35, Woolwich County Court

Over £16,000 was awarded and the tenant had not been evicted

This is not an HMO case. Here, the landlord failed to protect the deposit and there were repair problems with the boiler and windows.

However, it was the landlord's behaviour that was the main problem. The landlord made it clear that they did not want Mr. Newman, the tenant, in the property and had continually contacted the tenant asking him to leave.

The landlord tried to make the tenant sign a tenancy agreement for an extra £500 per month and attended the property without an appointment. He also reported the tenant to the police, saying that he had threatened to blow up the building. When the landlord issued proceedings for possession, Mr. Newman counterclaimed.

The judge awarded:

- £2,995 under the tenancy deposit regulations.

- £9,250 for disrepair (20% of rent between May 08 – Dec 09, 75% rent between Dec 08 and Jun 09, 43% rent from June onwards).

- £2,000 for harassment.

- £2,000 exemplary damages.

Total £16,250, plus the judge ordered that the landlord protect the deposit.

COMMENT

Again, this case goes to show how enormous compensation can mount up for chronic disrepair problems. There are insufficient details in the case to comment on the disrepair. A reference is made to windows and boiler, both would have cost less to repair than the compensation of £9,250 awarded. Why the tenant should not be expected to mitigate their loss is beyond me. In nearly every other field of law, the courts would expect the claimant to mitigate their loss. That is, to reduce the loss by taking reasonable action to stop the loss.

I also wonder what evidence of harassment there was that the landlord had *'continually contacted the tenant asking him to leave'*. How was this proved? It is not against the law to ask a tenant to leave once, it is illegal to continuously ask a tenant to leave.

It is not clear if the landlord managed to get possession and on what ground(s) he was trying to evict the tenant. Why had he not tried to evict the tenant legally? I can understand an inexperienced landlord would be put off by the cost of employing a solicitor to evict a tenant and to do it himself is intimidating. I suspect cases like this could be avoided if the eviction process was much simpler and easier to understand. Raising the rent is not a crime, it is perfectly legal providing the correct notice is used, though in this case the landlord went about it the wrong way.

The award of £2,998 under the Tenancy Deposit regulations and then to order the deposit to be protected seems strange and I suspect legally doubtful. The problem with the Tenancy Deposit Scheme is that it is appallingly badly drafted. I would have no part in it and refuse to take deposits. It was unfortunate that the largest landlord association promoted their own scheme and made a fortune out of running it, which I suspect blurred their minds as to the detail.

Abbas v Iqbal: 2009

Bow County Court, 4th June 2009, LAG August 2009

A room in an HMO case involving unlawful eviction, disrepair, and an award of £39,194

More than six years previous to this claim, the landlord granted Abbas, an elderly man, a weekly tenancy of a single room with shared use of bathroom and kitchen at a rent of £60 per week. In 2007, the landlord informed the tenants that he was going to convert the property into flats. In April 2008, the landlord gave the tenants two weeks' notice to terminate the tenancy, but this notice did not comply with the requirements of the Housing Act 1988.

In May, the gas and water were disconnected. In June, Abbas obtained an injunction against the landlord, requiring him to reinstate the utility supply. The landlord ignored this and building work continued. Within a week, the property was a shell and unsafe. Abbas was forced from the property and slept at friends' houses until the local authority re-housed him. The tenant's possessions, which remained in his room, were removed and disposed of.

The judge ruled against the landlord, assessing damages at £39,194 comprising of:

- £1,950 – 13 days at £150 per day for the period without utilities.

- £750 for the three days that the tenant had to sleep rough at £250 per day.

- £1,000 for having to leave before his tenancy had been terminated.

- £10,000 for aggravated damages.

- £7,500 for exemplary damages.

- £12,000 for cockroach and rodent infestation during the period of the tenancy.

- £500 – for 6-month period when the toilet was defective.

- £5,494 – special damages.

A total award of £39,194.

COMMENT

I am rarely in support of legal action against landlords, but I can find little to condone or excuse the behaviour of the landlord in this case after an injunction was served on him. Yes, he had given the tenant plenty of notice to leave but he had not followed the proper procedure, and to ignore an injunction was lunacy.

The level of damages awarded to the tenant is insane. £150 per day for not having utilities! People deprived of their liberty (unlawfully imprisoned) receive the same level of compensation. £20 per week compensation out of a weekly rent of £60 per week for a "toilet fault"!

Does this mean it did not flush? What's wrong with using a bucket to flush the toilet? It is debatable whether the infestation was the landlord's responsibility as rodents and cockroaches are attracted when food is left out. I suspect this was the tenant's fault, yet he was awarded £12,000 for something that he could have sorted out himself by contacting the council's environmental health department.

It would be interesting to find out what notice the landlord had received regarding these faults. I suspect the tenant had little evidence to show that he had reported them. My experience of court action is that everything the tenant says is believed, and nothing the landlord says is believed unless he can provide documented proof.

In some ways the landlord got off lightly when you compare this case to Oxford City Council v Kenton McIntosh, where the council prosecuted the landlord for illegal eviction and he was imprisoned for three months. You could also compare it to the Walsh v Shuangyan 2010, where the landlady was imprisoned for 28 days for disobeying an injunction. The enigma is that in the case of Abbas v Iqbal, the council did not instigate prosecution yet this is a more blatant abuse of tenant's rights, especially after the service of an injunction. Hardly an even-handed balanced approach. It seems justice is nothing more than a lottery.

Mental or Other Loss or Injury

If you think the compensation for disrepair seems bad, then see what happens if the tenant alleges he suffered mental harm or loss of employment as a result of eviction.

Hunt v Hussain: 2009

October 2009: Legal Action 25, Epson County Court

Psychiatric damages awarded following unlawful eviction; daily rate of damages limited to the period before the landlord would have lawfully been able to regain possession.

The defendants Mr. and Mrs. Hussain were husband and wife. In May 2003, Mr. Hussain granted Mr. Hunt an assured shorthold tenancy of a room at a weekly rent of £90. After three months, Mr. Hunt lost his job and needed to apply for Housing Benefit. Mrs. Hussain told him that he had to leave. The council wrote, warning her that she required a court order. Despite this, Mr. and Mrs. Hussain changed the locks and refused to re-admit him. Mr. Hunt, who was 45 years old, was made homeless and spent three months on the streets before he was able to secure alternative accommodation. Occasionally, he stayed with friends. Most of the time, he slept in a broken-down car or slept where he could in his sleeping bag. He suffered from bronchial asthma, which was made worse by living rough. He developed depression and feelings of self-harm.

Some four years after the eviction, a psychiatrist confirmed that he was suffering from severe depression, agoraphobia, and paranoid ideation. He was not fit to return to work and it was difficult to predict whether he would become fit for work in the future. The psychiatrist concluded that the trauma of the eviction on someone with his background and personality had generated this radical deterioration in his mental health. The local authority prosecuted Mrs. Hussain under the Protection from Eviction Act 1977 s1.

She was fined £300 and ordered to pay costs of £250. In civil proceedings, relying on breach of contract and tort, judgment in default was entered against Mr. and Mrs. Hussain. (*Judgment in default* means the defendant (landlord) did not defend the case).

The judge awarded damages totalling to £56,678 under the following heads:

- £8,125 for the eviction: damages were assessed at £125 per day over a period of 65 days. The judge was not willing to assess damages over the full period of 76 days that Mr Hunt was homeless on the grounds that Mr. and Mrs. Hussain could have lawfully terminated the tenancy by servicing a Housing Act 1988 s21 notice.

- £45,000 damages for personal injury. The judge had regard to the judicial studies board guidelines on awards for psychiatric damages. He also had regard to the adverse impact of the homelessness on Mr Hunt's asthma. The judge was satisfied that it fell into the most severe category of psychiatric damage for which the guideline amount is between £35,000 to £74,000.

- £100 special damages (£730 was claimed).

- £3,453 interest.

A total award of £56,678.

COMMENT

A truly terrifying case from a landlord's point of view in that such enormous compensation of £45,000 was obtained for what could be considered an *'unprovable injury'*, the existence and cause of mental trauma. The tenant, Hunt, lost his job in 2003 in the south of England. He later developed various psychiatric ailments. I am not commenting on him as an individual, but I find those who are inclined not to work will now complain of psychiatric problems such as depression, multiple personality, or bipolar disorder. HMO tenants are generally transient and rarely show much attachment to their property, certainly not during the early part of their occupation. The number of tenants I have who tell me, almost as a badge of honour, their psychiatric problems allow them to claim enhanced benefits does not help to reduce my scepticism.

That this case came six years after eviction is also troubling. Even though a tenant has six years to bring an action for unlawful eviction, actions for personal injury are usually limited to three years. I am not sure how Hunt was able to claim for personal injury (i.e. mental trauma) a full six years after eviction. I suspect that since the landlord did not defend the case, the time limit and the question whether trauma was actually provable was never examined. The fact that the landlords were warned by the local authority to evict using the proper process, then prosecuted, did not show them in a good light and they could be considered to have brought the matter on themselves.

The case is so extraordinary and a charter for *'no win, no fee'* solicitors that I am surprised there have not been more cases alleging mental trauma due to unlawful eviction. I would imagine it wouldn't be difficult to get a psychiatrist to certify that a tenant suffered mental trauma by being evicted, and the converse for a fee to get another psychiatrist to say the mental trauma was not due to the eviction, possibly nullifying or making this aspect of the claim unprovable. This case does not bode well for landlords who are not scrupulously careful when evicting tenants and those not able to mount a robust defence.

I find it odd that the judge had been exceedingly generous in allowing compensation for psychiatric damage, but only gave what is the lowest award I have seen for having to sleep rough due to being unlawfully evicted. He had done what no other judge I know had and limited the amount of compensation to the period the judge considered it would take to lawfully evict the tenant, just over nine weeks. Yes, you could get a possession order within nine weeks if you are lucky, but this time is not an average. In most cases, it takes longer. To me, this goes to show the closeted world judges inhabit.

It is surprising that it took the tenant 76 days to find alternative accommodation. The length of time some tenants allege it takes them to find accommodation after being unlawfully evicted cannot but raise questions. Sometimes it seems that the duty to mitigate, a well-known concept in law, has gone missing.

Arabhalvaei v Rezaeipoor: 2008

January 2008: Legal Action 36 Central London County Court

£188,000 damages for harassment and disrepair

This is not an HMO case. Mr. Rezaeipoor was a protected tenant of a one-bedroom flat which he shared with his wife from 1995 until January 2006. A protected tenant is a pre-1988 tenancy covered by the Rents Acts which gives a life tenancy and restricts the amount that can be charged. Mr. Rezaeipoor and his wife suffered as a result of disrepair at the flat and harassment from the claimant, the landlord, Arbhalvaei. The disrepair included penetrating damp, cracks to various internal walls, a leaking toilet and sink. The heating system was out of order at various times over the period in question, with the result that the property was without heating and hot water. The harassment comprised of verbal abuse, disconnecting of the water supply, nuisance telephone calls, locks to the property being filled with glue and on one occasion, a window being smashed with a bottle. The landlord ignored four statutory abatement notices served by the authority in respect of the disrepair, and letters from Mr. Rezaeipoor's Tenancy Relations Officer warning him that his action could amount to harassment. In 2000, Mr. Rezaeipoor lost his job as a radio presenter with BBC's world service as he was finding it increasingly difficult to leave his wife alone in the property. In 2004, the claimant issued possession proceedings based on rent arrears, and Mr. Rezaeipoor counterclaimed for damages for harassment and disrepair. In August 2007, the claimant's (the landlord's) claim was struck out and the claimant was debarred for defending the counterclaim.

The judge awarded damage of £184,026.21, calculated as follows:

- £22,500 for disrepair (50 percent of the rental value of £455 per month over the period in question).

- £46,500 for harassment (at a rate of £6,000 per annum).

- £67,500 for loss of employment.

- £2,601.68 special damages.

- £2,325 for additional special damages for heating, cleaning, and related damages.

- £5,000 for aggravated damages.

- £500 for exemplary damages.

- £37,099.53 interest.

Total award of £184,026.21.

COMMENT

This is the largest award for unlawful eviction I have seen and illustrates the reason institutional investors are reluctant to become residential landlords and also puts off risk-averse people from being landlords. Institutional investors (insurance companies) like to own offices, shopping markets, and would love to invest in residential property but have largely kept clear of buying residential investments because, amongst other things, they fear disrepair claims and the problems caused by evictions. This case shows that compensation can exceed the cost of the average house.

What I feel goes against the landlord is that he had FOUR abatement notices served upon him. Abatement notices are notices to repair property or to stop harassing the tenant. The landlord also had letters from the council's Tenancy Relations Officers, so he could not say that he didn't know what was going on. There was third party evidence, unlike cases like Murray v Kelly 2008, Abbas v Iqbal 2009, and Fakhari v Newman 2010 where there appears to be no third party evidence of disrepair. Those other cases give great concern because of the fact that the landlords could say the complaints of disrepair came out of the blue. It is a common occurrence that a tenant will say everything is okay until you serve them with an eviction notice. That's when a whole load of complaints of disrepair follow or they amazingly they fall down or up the stairs and start demanding compensation for personal injury.

The disrepair alleged in this case is also suspect:

Penetrating damp – This usually comes with allegations of green or black mould. I have never come across a case of damp, since it is always caused by lifestyle – i.e. lack of ventilation or heat, and it is an increasing complaint due to properties being sealed up. Old properties need to breathe. Tenants will not accept it is their responsibility to ventilate, heat the property, and clean off the mould.

Cracks – Without more details, it is difficult to come to any conclusions. Old houses move and this causes cracks, especially in London which is built on a clay basin. The clay shrinks during long dry periods and expands when it gets wet. Needless to say that this leads to subsidence and cracking.

In most cases, this is nothing more than a cosmetic problem, yet tenants do not understand the problem or choose not to and say that the property is falling down on them.

Leaking toilets and sinks – Leaks are also a common complaint and usually include showers and baths. Tenants often do not take responsibility and do not carry out any preventative measure, allowing a minor leak to ruin the floor and ceiling below. I have seen infestations of dry rot caused by a long-standing leak. All of this could have been avoided by putting a container underneath the leak and regularly emptying it. Some of my worse leaks have been caused by misuse like overfilling a bath or allowing hair to block the shower, and then allowing the water to flood over and cause devastation below. With old houses moving, leaks due to the movement are inevitable and landlords need to carry out regular checks as tenants will sometimes not take responsibility for reporting the situation.

Boilers – Boilers often have intermittent faults that are hard to identify. A common problem is the cost of heating, and so you have the allegation that it costs too much to heat the property therefore the boiler must be faulty.

There seems to be no completely satisfactory solution to disrepair allegations even though contemporaneous written records and regular inspection will reduce the likelihood of the claims being successful. In order to protect themselves, a prudent landlord should carry out regular property inspections, and get the tenant to sign an agreement that the premises are in satisfactory condition to reduce the likelihood of the tenant then alleging disrepair. Also, keep a written record of all requests and responses to repairs.

The other aspect of concern with this case is the award for loss of employment consisting of £67,500. The cause and effect does not seem to be clear. There are other causes for concern. Mental deterioration was surprisingly not claimed. There seems to be no limit as to what can be claimed once harassment or unlawful eviction is established and it can, as is shown here, go back for years. Claims are statute barred after six years (three years with personal injury) yet the award for harassment was for seven and three-quarter years (£6,000 pa, total award £46,500). The disrepair award is for about eight and a quarter years (£22,500 ÷ £455/2) – this is again questionable.

What is troubling about the case is that the landlord was prevented from defending the tenants' claims, so everything that the tenant claimed went unchallenged. Why the landlord was prevented from defending is not stated. In most cases, it is because the landlord was acting unreasonably and not complying with the court's directions to supply evidence. However, it is unbelievable that such a record award should not be scrutinised. I find the award of special damages of £2,601.58 without any justification questionable. Furthermore, to attribute to the landlord a bottle smashing the window and the locks being glued strikes me as strange. Also, the water supply being disconnected may not be down to the landlord – and if it was, there may have been a good reason for it. Heating systems break down and take time to repair; it does not mean that it was the landlord's fault.

Overall, a frightening case from a landlord's perspective and it emphasises that landlords need to be very careful in order to try and prevent such a situation. This includes obeying abatement notices and keep good records.

Obtaining a Possession Order or a Tenant Saying They Have Left

A possession order or the expiry of an eviction notice to quit does not allow the landlord to remove the tenant. An application to have the bailiff is required to remove the tenant. Then if the tenant refuses to go, they must be removed by a bailiff.

Naveed v Raja: 2007

July 2007: Legal Action 32 Willesden County Court

£27,000 aggravated and exemplary damages where the tenant was assaulted

This is not an HMO case. Mr. Naveed was an assured shorthold tenant. In December 2005, he was injured in a car accident and had no means of paying his rent. He asked the defendant, his landlord, to provide him with a new tenancy agreement so that he could claim Housing Benefit. The defendant refused and instead served a Housing Act 1988 s21 notice. On the day that the notice expired, the defendant's father, who was managing the property and three other men assaulted the claimant and evicted him. They took all his property. He slept for three nights in a car. After obtaining an injunction, he was readmitted to the property, but his belongings were not returned. Three weeks later, he was again assaulted by three men, one of whom had been with the defendant's father on the previous occasion. Mr. Naveed was beaten with sticks and sustained injuries to his head, body, and legs. He was kept in the hospital overnight. He was too scared to return to the property.

The judge awarded:

- £10,000 general damages.

- £15,000 aggravated and exemplary damages.

- £2,000 special damages for lost possessions.

A total award of £27,000.

COMMENT

There is no breakdown of how the compensation is calculated and to give £25,000 for general aggravated and exemplary damages is excessive. I am in no way excusing the assault, though in mitigation the landlord had followed the legal process except where the tenant refused to go, then a bailiff should have been used. Unless the whole process is used, it seems to make little difference to the court – it is all or nothing!

I find it odd that even if a court order is given and the tenant refuses to leave, they are not held as accountable as the landlord. If a landlord disobeys a court order, they can be sent to prison. See Walsh v Shuangyan 2010 where the landlord was sent to prison for 28 days for disobeying a court order, yet a tenant appears to be able to ignore a court order with impunity.

If you compare this case with Odera v Iqbal 2010 (where a child was assaulted, though the assault was not as severe as this case) only £2,500 was awarded. That's one-tenth of what Raja received. It is quite bizarre! The fact that the tenant could get an injunction to be readmitted also seems unfair after a valid notice had expired.

It only goes to show how precious the courts are and how unfair the system is about following procedure and how biased it is against landlords. Maybe it's simply a matter of how good the tenant's lawyer was or how bad the landlord's defence was. There is no way to determine this from the report.

Even if the tenant says they have left, this may not be conclusive.

Odera v Iqbal: 2010

January 2010 Legal Action 33 Luton County Court

This is an HMO case. The claimant was the assured shorthold tenant of a room in a three-bedroom house with shared, communal amenities. From August 2007, she lived there with her 11-year-old daughter. The defendant was the landlord. There was no written agreement. Ms. Odera claimed that throughout her tenancy, the defendant harassed her by entering the premises unannounced and without warning. In January 2008, he gave her a defective notice seeking possession. She began looking for alternative accommodation. On 17th February 2008, she packed her belongings and told the defendant that she was on her way to collect the keys for her new accommodation. However, the new landlord would not give her the keys to the promised accommodation as her deposit was short by £60. She returned to the premises about 8pm.

Later that night, the defendant and another man removed the tenant's belongings and placed them outside the front of the property. He dragged both the claimant and her daughter out of the bedroom, down the stairs, and outside. They remained there for approximately an hour and a half. Although the police were called, they accepted the defendant's word that the claimant had no right to remain in the premises, but requested that he store her belongings until she could collect them the next day. She spent the night in emergency accommodation and then stayed with her sister in Watford for three days. When the claimant returned to the premises to collect her belongings, she discovered that they had been discarded in the back garden and were soaked and rain-damaged.

The judge accepted the claimant's evidence. He found that she had been subject to harassment from the defendant after the expiry of the invalid notice to quit on 6th February until her eviction on 17th February. The judge accepted that the claimant and her daughter were assaulted.

He found that although the claimant had hoped to, was ready to, and intended to vacate the premises, she had not formally surrendered the tenancy. She had not handed over the keys and did not make any unequivocal act amounting to surrender.

The judge accepted that her belongings were damaged in the way alleged. He ordered an enquiry concerning damages for the value of the belongings, to be subject of a later hearing. In the interim, he awarded general damages.

The judge awarded:

- £500 for breach of covenant for quiet enjoyment and trespass for the two weeks before eviction.

- £1,000 for the assault and method of eviction.

- £1,500 aggravated damages, particularly given that the claimant's daughter witnessed and was subject to an assault.

- £1,000 exemplary damages because the defendant sought to increase his income by obtaining new tenants who could pay the full rent for the entirety of the premises.

- Subsequently, the parties agreed to a figure of £750 by way of special damages.

A total award of £4,750.

COMMENT

A disgraceful way to treat a mother and her eleven-year-old daughter, even if you think you are in the right. However, it appears that the landlord believed the tenant had left. If the reverse was argued, and the landlord had tried to sue for rent saying the tenant had not left as she had not given back the keys, I doubt the landlord would have succeeded. What could only be described as a technicality in not having the keys back made all the difference, resulting in an award against the landlord of £4,750. I suspect the legal cost would be very much more than this. I think the landlord has got off lightly in this case with aggravated damages of only £1,500 if you compare it with the case of Naveed v Raja 2007 where £15,000 was awarded, admittedly for a much more severe assault but no children were involved. Also, no general damages were awarded for the period the tenant was homeless. This could have been as much as £300 per day, and possibly more as a child was also homeless. Or maybe not – see Deelah v Rehman 2010 where a whole family were only awarded £250 per day.

I would imagine the landlord now wishes he had given the tenant the £60 she was short. However, if he is like many landlords I know, then he believes that money only flows one way – into his pocket!

In such circumstances, I would advise a landlord to back off. Unless you have the keys and a signed letter from the tenant saying they've left, and have left taking their possessions, you need to be very, very careful. In such circumstances, I have *'lent'* (you never get it back) the tenant the money providing I got the keys, they signed a release form and they left after taking everything with them, or agreed in writing that what was left were things they did not want.

Keddey v Hughes: 2010

Just because a tenant says they are leaving does not mean they have to leave

This is not an HMO case. Mr. Keddey lived in a property with his mother from 2005, and took it over for himself in mid-2007. The landlord believed that Mr. Keddey had agreed to move out in October 2008 and arranged to let the property to new tenants. However, Mr. Keddey then decided not to move.

The owner assaulted Mr. Keddey on a number of occasions and then physically ejected him from the property, although he was able to get back in later that day.

Later in the month, Mr. Keddey came home to find the landlord in his property, packing up his furniture. Some of his possessions were damaged. Mr. Keddey decided to leave and not return. He stayed in bed and breakfast accommodation for three or four weeks before finding alternative accommodation.

The judge awarded:

- £4,620 for unlawful eviction, being £165 per night for the 28 days in B&B.

- £1,500 for harassment and trespass to person and property.

- £1,000 for aggravated damages.

- £2,000 exemplary damages, as the ejection from the property had been public, upsetting, and humiliating. Furthermore, the defendant had been warned by the local authority not to do it. Plus the rent charged to the new tenants was more than that charged to Mr. Keddey.

A total awarded of £9,120.

COMMENT

Overall, a fairly low award given the circumstances, due to the tenant finding new accommodation within three or four weeks. Odd that the tenant could not be more precise about the time it took to find new accommodation, yet he was awarded general damages for four weeks at £165 per night for living in a B&B. Though this case is consistent with Ogle v Bundhoo: 2009, it still seems like an excessive sum of money to give for the privilege of living in a B&B. However, only £1,500 for harassment and assault appears slightly on the low side particularly as assault is alleged. I believe that the court in this case mixed up aggravated damages given for upset and distress, with exemplary damages, which are usually given for avoiding the cost of eviction and or the profit made by evicting the tenant.

Harassment

Wandsworth Council v Ace Lettings: 2011

A Wimbledon-based firm of property agents were fined after conducting a campaign of harassment against some of its tenants. The company was ordered to pay £20,561 after Wandsworth Council took it to court.

The case revealed that the property agents had turned off the water and electricity, damaged the toilet facilities, sealed up letterboxes, and sent builders to the property without notice, who then left the property full of rubble and rubbish.

The front door locks were also changed, the tenants' belongings were packed up and removed from the house and the tenants were told to leave without being presented with an official eviction notice.

Paul Ellis, Wandsworth Council member for Housing, said, "This was a truly shocking and relentless campaign of harassment and intimidation carried out against innocent tenants."

COMMENT

This was a criminal case and it's interesting to compare what the civil courts have awarded for harassment – usually far less.

See Deelah v Rehman: 2011 – where £1,500 was awarded.

See Walsh v Shuangyan: 2010 – where £2,000 was awarded.

See Lord and Haslewood – Orgam v Jessop: 1999 where £1,000 was awarded.

See Fakhari v Newman: 2010 where £2,000 was awarded.

See Arabhalvaei v Rezaeipoor: 2008 where £46,500 was awarded.

It is rare to see cases on harassment. This case resulted in a criminal conviction and a heavy fine for the agent. The conviction could also have serious implications for the agent from a professional point of view, which might have resulted in them going out of business. If they belonged to a professional body, they could have their membership terminated for gross misconduct.

We have only heard one side of the case: the council's. It would be interesting to hear the agent's story. I wonder if it would sound like this: "The tenant who was in substantial arrears asked for the repairs to be done and then started to complain about the disturbance and the builders. The tenants said they would leave, but changed their mind."

The case illustrates the excessive fines that are given by the courts are disproportionate to other fines for criminal activity. The fine is paid to the state, thus the tenant does not receive any of it. This seems strange since it's the tenant who has suffered the harm, not the state. Criminal action is designed to deter such behaviour. The cost of prosecution is increasingly being claimed against the landlord and it is believed that some councils have ramped up prosecution as a way of covering staff costs. Note that the tenant can also bring a civil action against the agent or landlord and receive compensation which they can keep. The likelihood is that the agents or landlord have agreed a private settlement over the civil liability for harassment. Also appreciate that in a civil action the landlord is liable for the actions of the agent and will have to compensate the tenant, even though the landlord had not harassed the tenant.

HMO Daddy runs courses on DIY eviction and shows you how you can simply, quickly, cheaply & legally evict tenants with any rent arrears without the need for expensive lawyers.

PLEASE VISIT MY WEBSITE

www.hmodaddy.com

Appendix

1. Glossary of legal terms used in the book

2. Applying rent to pay for repairs

3. Licences and ASTs

Appendix 1:
Glossary of Legal Terms Used

Abandonment:

This is where a tenant leaves without giving notice or surrendering their tenancy. The courts are reluctant to recognise abandonment without clear evidence that the tenant intended to leave.

Article 4:

An area where planning permission is needed for a small HMO. For most of England and Wales, planning permission is not needed *'for up to 6 sharing'*. An Article 4 area is where planning permission is needed for more than two sharers. Contact your local council to see if it applies in your area.

Assured Shorthold Tenancy (AST):

This is the standard tenancy used in the private sector where the landlord can regain possession of the property six months after the beginning of the tenancy or the original length of the tenancy, whichever is longer, as long as they provide the tenant with two months' notice.

Bailiff:

A court official who is authorised to remove tenants from properties after a 'possession order' has expired. Only a court bailiff can remove a tenant.

Case:

Civil law has partly developed by litigants going to court and disputing the matter. The case is named after the litigants and the date is the year the case was recorded in the law reports. For example, in Deelah v Rehman: 2011, Deelah is the tenant and Rehman is the landlord. The date is when the case was recorded, usually the year of the trial. The 'v' is pronounced 'and' not versus - 'versus' or 'against' is used in criminal cases.

Civil law:

A set of rights and obligations imposed by law and enforceable by individuals against each other.

Claimant:

The person in a civil matter who brings about a court action. Previously referred to as a *plaintiff* and is usually (but not always) the first named person in the case.

Committal proceedings:

An application to the court in a civil matter to imprison a person who is in breach of a court order, usually an injunction.

Complainant:

The person in a civil matter who brings about a court action. Previously referred to as a *plaintiff* and is usually (but not always) the first named person in the case.

Contempt of court:

If a person breaches a court order then they are said to be in contempt of court. This is usually the result of breaking an 'injunction' and can result in the offender being fined and/or being sent to prison. See Walsh v Shuangyan: 2010.

Criminal law:

Obligations imposed by the state and enforced by state officials such as the police and/or trading standards officers.

Damages:

The word that lawyers use for compensation. The courts reduce all losses down to a financial sum of money which is paid to the complainant. Distinguished from a *'fine'*, which a criminal court awards and is paid to the state.

Defendant:

The person who is being sued by the *'complainant'*. It is usually (but not always) the second name in the name of a case.

Duty to mitigate:

In civil law, the *'complainant'* is under an obligation to take reasonable steps to reduce their loss. This includes steps like protecting goods and finding alternative work. In landlord and tenant cases, this duty seems to be ignored by the courts and there appears to be no obligation on a tenant to carry out or appoint someone to carry out repairs to their property or to find alternative accommodation quickly if they are unlawfully evicted.

Fine:

A fine is one of the most common punishments the criminal courts award and is paid to the state, unlike *'damages'* which are paid to the claimant. Non-lawyers often get confused by this. Money is money. The victim of a crime may have the satisfaction of seeing the offender prosecuted and if the offender is fined, the victim does not get the fine paid to them. The money goes to the state and not to the wronged individual. The state appears to be making money out of the victim's misfortune. In cases when the victim suffers physical and mental injury from an assault or attack, they can apply for compensation from the government. The government does not provide any compensation for damages or loss of property. Unless the victim is insured, they get nothing.

Harassment:

This is a civil and criminal offence and is defined as anything which interferes with a tenant's quiet enjoyment of their tenancy. Regularly contacting the tenant is such an example if the tenant does not want the landlord to do so. More blatant examples are cutting off utilities and gluing up locks.

HMO:

Houses in Multiple Occupation, also known as multi-lets or shared housing. Under the Housing Act 2004, it means a house let to three or more unrelated persons.

Housing Benefit:

A system where the state pays for the housing of unemployed and low paid tenants. Tenants on housing benefit are often referred to as Benefit, DSS, DWP or LHA tenants.

Injunction:

A court order in civil proceedings which states that if the party it is addressed to does not comply, they are said to be in *'contempt of court'* and the court can *'fine'* the party or even send them to prison. An injunction *'ex parte'* or *'without notice'* means it is obtained without the defendant knowing or being able to object until after it is granted.

Judgment:

The court decision. Note that the 'e' is missing after the 'g' in a court judgment.

Law reports:

Some courts' decisions that are considered significant are recorded. There are many different law reports and they are provided by private companies, though most can be viewed online for no cost.

Licence to occupy:

An alternative form of the right to occupy property, similar to an 'AST' and still requires a court order to remove the tenant.

Plaintiff:

The old word for claimant or complainant.

Possession order:

This is an order of the court which requires a tenant to leave a property. A residential occupier cannot be removed from a property without a court order, unless they voluntarily leave. This is known as *'surrender'*. If a landlord attempts to remove a tenant without a court order, they have committed a criminal and civil offence.

Section 8:

Under the Housing Act 1988, there are 17 grounds given by section 8 which allow a landlord, if they have the specified cause, to apply to the courts to remove a tenant. In practice, only one ground is used. That is ground 8, which is that the tenant is 8 weeks (if paid weekly) or 2 months (if rent is paid monthly) in arrears of rent. The landlord has the right if the tenant is over 8 weeks or 2 months arrears to serve a notice, which must comply with specific requirements, giving a minimum of at least 2 weeks' notice that they intend to apply to the court to get a *'possession order'*. Unlike 'section 21', (below) a landlord can commence an application for a possession order as soon as any of the *'grounds'* given under section 8 apply.

Section 21:

Under the Housing Act 1988, the landlord can apply to the court to remove any 'AST' tenant without *'grounds'* by giving 2 month's notice. This notice must be correctly written. The tenant has the right to occupy under an AST for at least 6 months, longer if the tenancy agreement is for longer than 6 months, before a section 21 action can commence. It does not matter that the tenant is in breach of their tenancy, for example, not paying the rent. A section 21 guarantees the tenant a minimum of six months' occupation plus the time it takes for the court to process an application, which is usually 6 – 9 weeks. If the tenant does not leave, the time it takes the bailiff to remove the tenant can be added to this timeframe. It usually takes anywhere between 2 to 6 weeks for a bailiff to remove a tenant.

Surrender:

This is where the tenant clearly shows that they have left the property. It requires the tenant to leave and normally hand the keys back to the landlord.

Appendix 2:
Applying Rent to Pay for Repairs

There is a common law right established in the case of Lee-Parker v Izzett 1971 to use money due as rent to pay for repairs. However, a tenant must use the following steps:

1. Give the landlord notice of the need for repairs in writing.

2. If, after a reasonable period has elapsed, the repairs have still not been done, write again telling the landlord of the intention to arrange the repairs and deduct the cost from the rent.

3. Obtain estimates for the cost of the work from at least two reputable contractors and write again enclosing copies of the estimates and giving the landlord a deadline to carry out the work, failing which the tenant will arrange for the works to be done and deduct the cost from the rent.

4. If there is no response from the landlord, arrange for the work to be done by the contractor who submitted the lowest estimate, obtaining receipts showing the extent of the works.

5. Send the landlord a copy of the receipts and explain exactly how the rent deduction will be made, or has been made, so as to cover the cost of the work.

6. Shelter, the housing charity, strangely enough has always seemed to look upon tenants as victims. They encourage tenants to do repairs themselves. See www.shelter.com

Appendix 3:
Licences v ASTs

The issues of letting by using licences instead of ASTs has recently become a hot topic with some councils.

Many HMO landlords use licences instead of the traditional ASTs (Assured Shorthold Tenancies) when letting. Why? Because it gives HMO landlords greater control over their tenants. With certain types of tenants, usually at the lower end of the market, this is often a requirement. The other reason is that it is often wrongly thought it is easier to evict a licensee.

Whatever you call the agreement, in law it is what it is. If the tenant has exclusive possession, even of a room in a shared house, and it is used as the occupier's primary or main residence then it will be an AST, regardless of what the agreement is called.

It is generally known by most landlords that AST tenants can only be evicted by a court order if they refuse to leave. This is true even if they are refusing to pay their rent and/or damaging the property. What is not usually appreciated is that the same applies to a residential licensee. If a licensee refuses to go, then a court order is required to remove the licensee.

The reason that licensees are easier in practice to deal with is because they usually leave when asked. Many Tenancy Support Officers also do not know that a court order is required for a licensee and unlike ASTs where they have been known to tell the tenants that it is their 'right' and often encourage the tenant to stay put and not pay the rent until the bailiff evicts them, they do not give licensees the same advice.

Even Shelter, the housing charity, get this wrong if you check their very clear website where they have a checklist asking: Are You a Tenant? If you follow it, it appears to say that a licensee in a shared house can be asked to leave without a court order. See www.shelter.co.uk

Evicting a licensee who refuses to leave is a relatively straightforward process, even though it takes a lot of time and involves a fee. You do not need any reason; you just have to use a valid notice giving 28 days' notice ending on a rent day. If the licensee still has not left, then you need to pay £280 for the summons (it is only £250 to evict an AST for rent arrears if you do it online). It takes about 8 weeks to get a court hearing (usually 5 weeks online for an AST if you evict for rent arrears) and the judge normally gives the licensee another 14 days to leave. If the licensee still has not left, then a court bailiff is required. This can take anywhere between two weeks to a couple of months depending on how busy they are. Rapid Evictions Ltd provides a very cost efficient eviction service for both types of tenants and also eviction packs for evicting both licensees and ASTs. See www.rapideviction.com

Legally, there is very little difference between using an AST and a licence when it comes to evicting tenants. So I wonder why many Housing Standard Officers get so upset about landlords using licences. The Housing Officers have never explained why they get upset about the use of licences. They get very defensive when I point out that they use licences with their own HMOs and hostels and they can, unlike the private sector, evict at will. In other words, they can evict a tenant without going to court. There is so much hypocrisy out there. We are policed by our competitors who often ignore their own massive failings with their own housing and get very aggressive about *'faults'* with properties in the private sector, which rarely stand up to any scientific analysis as to why they are *'faults'*. Such behaviour, though indefensible, is the system you have to put up with if you wish to be a landlord.

There is also a misunderstanding out there about *'Serviced Accommodation'*, *'Short Term Lets'*, *'B&Bs and Hotels'*. Many think such accommodation provides no security of tenure, meaning that an occupier can be evicted without a court order or notice. This is not legally correct. The key to all this is the Protection from Eviction Act 1977 Section 3A, which states that *'Excluded Occupiers'* or *'Excluded Tenancies'* are the only people who can be asked to leave without a court order, but *'reasonable notice'* is required. Excluded Occupiers or Excluded Tenancies are:

- Resident landlords with shared accommodation.

- Licences granted to trespassers.

- Holiday lets.

- Rent-free accommodation in the public sector.

- Accommodation provided to asylum-seekers.

The Prevention from Eviction Act 1977 Section 3 states that a court order is required to evict all other tenants, residential occupiers, or residential licensees. This includes those not listed in Section 3 A in (8) above, however short their stay. Getting it wrong can result in enormous - and I suggest, disproportional - compensation being awarded. See the cases outlined throughout this book.

With *'Serviced Accommodation', 'Short Term Lets', 'B&Bs and Hotels'* it all depends on how the tenant is occupying. If it is their permanent residence, they will fall within the Prevention from Eviction Act 1977 and require a court order.

As you can see, this is not an easy topic and you can understand why so many get it wrong. Why are councils now focusing on the tenure and becoming concerned about the use of 'licensees'? I believe it is because there are many who work for councils who wish to destroy or restrict the private sector. It goes hand-in-hand with licensing of properties, Article 4, increased housing standards especially amenity standards within HMOs. Councils are annoyed that the planning controls on HMOs have been removed allowing up to six 'sharing'. This previously did a lot to restrict the supply of HMOs. By the way, the council's idea of control is to prevent HMOs from being established.

Councils have now woken up to the fact they have many other weapons with which to attack the private sector; one being that if they can encourage enough tenants not to pay their rent and stay put until the bailiffs evict (which can take up to six months) then how many landlords can afford this? Even better, how many landlords are going to be discouraged from entering this market? The councils will retort that they are only applying the law, but as anyone who is aware of the situation can determine, most 'law' is ignored or is said to be 'decriminalised'. So why emphasise this law? Because councils do not always act in the best interest of private landlords.

The Author

HMO Daddy, Jim Haliburton, is a star of the BBC show *'Meet The Landlords'*, author of over 10 books and manuals including *How to Become a Multi-Millionaire HMO Landlord* and regularly writes articles for property magazines.

He began investing in property in 1991, letting rooms to students while he was a college law lecturer.

By 2004, he decided to leave his job and buy investment properties full-time. He now owns a letting office, as well as over 100 HMOs, 30 single-lets, and has 24 Rent-to-Rents.

He is also in regular demand as a speaker at property meetings around the UK, and runs courses and mentorships on the business of being an HMO landlord. He is unique in the business in that he lets people work in his property business to learn the skills of being an HMO landlord and gives tours of his properties.

I Want to Hear From You

As a reader of the first edition of my case book, you are the most important critic and commentator. I value your opinion and comments and want to know what else you would like me to include, what you disagree with, and any other words of wisdom you wish to make.

I welcome your views. You can email, call or write to me to let me know what you did or did not like about my casebook, as well as what I can do to make my case book better or what other information or service I could provide. Please note that I am often difficult to contact by phone because, as you can appreciate, I am very busy, but when I get a few spare minutes I love to talk about the business so please do not be offended if I say call back or leave a message.

If you are interested in finding out more, I also provide training courses on all aspects of the business including how to evict tenants quickly, easily, cheaply and above all **LEGALLY**. I have also written the only manual there is on how to evict tenants yourself. It's called *DIY Eviction* and you can find on my website www.hmodaddy.com

When you write to me, please include your name and email address. Your home address and phone number would also help. I assure you I will value and review your comments.

Email: jim@hmodaddy.com

Website: www.hmodaddy.com

Mail: Jim Haliburton
       14 Walsall Road
       Wednesbury
       WS10 9JL

Phone: 09131-300054

Calls cost £1.50 per minute